5.⁰⁰

# COACHING FOOTBALL FOR YOUNG ATHLETES

# COACHING FOOTBALL FOR YOUNG ATHLETES

TOM
CAPOZZOLI

**Contemporary Books, Inc.**
Chicago

**Library of Congress Cataloging in Publication Data**

Capozzoli, Tom, 1927–
    Coaching football for young athletes.

    Includes index.
    1. Football coaching.    2. School sports.
I. Title.
GV956.6.C36        796.332′07′7        80-16997
ISBN 0-8092-7010-2
ISBN 0-8092-7009-9 (pbk.)

*Dedication:*
To all the Doms who "loved it."

Published by Contemporary Books, Inc.
180 North Michigan Avenue, Chicago, Illinois 60601
Manufactured in the United States of America
Library of Congress Catalog Card Number: 80-16997
International Standard Book Number: 0-8092-7010-2 (cloth)
                                    0-8092-7009-9 (paper)

Published simultaneously in Canada by
Beaverbooks
953 Dillingham Road
Pickering, Ontario L1W 1Z7
Canada

# Contents

To my assistant coaches for all of their support;
to my family and friends for their good wishes;
and to the expert typing effort that was performed.

# Foreword

Much has been said about the value of athletics. It builds strong bodies, develops character, and provides fun and excitement. The joy of victory is great but sometimes even the sadness of defeat can help a boy develop into a normal young man.

In order to get the most out of any sport, a boy must be prepared. He must learn how to perform the physical tasks each sport requires. Therefore, it is necessary for him to prepare his body for the game he likes and to sharpen the skills that will enable him to compete with other players.

To help him learn how to play football, he must be coached by men who are qualified to instruct him in the techniques required at each position. There are many men who have the time and interest to coach but have not had sufficient experience or training to qualify as capable instructors. Although this sport has developed over the years into a very complex game, it can be played very simply with a basic approach geared to the age and skills of the participants.

This book will address the basic aspects of the game and will attempt to prepare interested men for coaching young boys. It contains material that is appropriate for football programs at all levels: lower (ages 9–11), intermediate (ages 12–14), and upper levels (15 and above). It will go into some detail about every phase of offensive and defensive play, giving performance requirements for each position and describing how a coach should help a young boy develop his ability to play football. Further on in the book the material broadens to provide more extensive information that is particularly useful to high school teams. Because boys are different, each boy and his coaches must decide which position he should play. The physical requirements of each position will be reviewed to enable them to determine which position a boy can best qualify for.

It is important to remember that having fun is the best reason to play any game. In order to have more fun, you must strive to win. This book should help you get ready to win.

# 1

# The Game

Football is considered to be one of the most exciting sports in America. It abounds at all age levels, beginning with youngsters below ten years of age and on up to collegiate and professional ranks. Its popularity is based on the excitement surrounding the blocking and tackling, running and passing of the players on each team as they attempt to outscore each other.

Each team is permitted to put eleven players on the field. They take turns at offensive play (trying to score) and defensive play (trying to prevent scores). The game begins with the toss of a coin by the officials who administer the game and enforce its rules. New coaches must obtain rulebooks to become familiar with the regulations governing the game in order to instruct their players. The team winning the toss may elect to receive or kick the opening kickoff.

The referee, the official in charge of the game, places the ball on the kicking team's 40-yard line

and, with the ball propped up on a kicking tee, the defensive team's kicker and his ten teammates race down the field after the kick to tackle the offensive team's ball carrier. After the tackle, the referee places the ball at the spot of the tackle, directs the ten-yard chain holders to put one end of the chain parallel with the ball, and signals the ball ready for play.

From that point, the offense must gain ten yards on four attempts (called "downs") in order to retain the ball. "First down and 10 to go" is the referee's call when the ball has been advanced beyond the other end of the chain. The offense may maintain ball control all the way down the field until they score or fail to make the ten yards. A touchdown is the main way to score and may happen by either running the ball across the goal line or passing it to a teammate beyond the goal into the end zone. If a team fails to make a touchdown, it may elect

1

OPENING KICKOFF. An exciting game begins before a packed house; seventy-seven thousand people rise to their feet.

TOUCHDOWN! There's no greater thrill for a football player.

to try a field goal, which is a place kick through the goal posts. All of these subjects will be covered in detail later in the book.

## OFFENSIVE TEAM

Football is an exciting game. Eleven players on one team try to run and pass the ball until they get it across the other team's goal line. The team with the ball is called the offensive team; the other eleven players who are trying to stop them are called the defensive team. Football, then, is a game of offense and defense.

The offense must have seven players called linemen. They are called linemen because they start each play on a line even with the ball. The other four players are called backfield men because they start in back of the linemen.

The seven offensive linemen play different positions which are known by different names. There is a center, two guards, two tackles, and two ends. The center is in the middle of the line and is responsible for centering or "snapping" the ball through his legs to the quarterback or other backfield men.

The two players on either side of the center are called guards. They must protect and guard the center and the "backs" (backfield men are called "backs") from any defensive player who tries to break through the linemen to tackle the backs. They must be strong and quick.

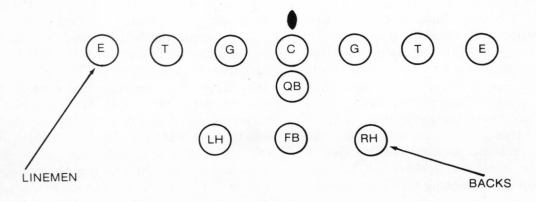

LINEMEN

BACKS

```
                    ●
                   Ball
   (G)             (C)             (G)
  Guard           Center          Guard
```

The two players outside the guards are known as tackles. They are usually bigger than guards because their job is to block the defensive team's best tacklers who play against them on the other side of the line of scrimmage (which is the boundary line between the offensive team and defensive team).

```
                   ●
                  Ball
  (T)    (G)     (C)     (G)    (T)
 Tackle                        Tackle
```

The last players on the offensive line are called ends because they are on the end of the line. Their job is also to block defensive players and to run down the field to catch a forward pass thrown by a back (usually the quarterback). They are usually tall, fast players who must also have the skill to catch the ball while running.

```
                   ●
                  Ball
 (E)   (T)   (G)  (C)  (G)   (T)   (E)
 End                              End
```

In order to better identify the offensive linemen, we refer to the players on the left side of the center as left guard, left tackle, and left end. On the other side of the center, the players are the right guard, right tackle, and right end.

OFFENSIVE AND DEFENSIVE STANCES. Center and both offensive guards are set to block middle guard and left and right middle linebackers.

The spacing (distance between) of the offensive linemen is sometimes different because of the kind of offensive play that is used. Here is an example.

The offense begins with a huddle, which is a team meeting on the field. The quarterback, who is the team's leader on the field, tells the team that they are going to try to run the ball outside of their left end. This would be more difficult to do if the offensive line was spread out because it would reduce the distance between the left end and the line at the side of the field (called the sideline). It would also force the defensive line to spread out and prevent the play from gaining yards. Therefore, the offensive line should squeeze closer together when the play called by the quarterback (QB) is going outside. There are many other things to be covered about line splits (spacing of linemen); these will be reviewed later.

The backs are usually known by four names. They are the quarterback (QB), left halfback

| (E) | (T) | (G) | (C) | (G) | (T) | (E) |
|---|---|---|---|---|---|---|
| Left | Left | Left | Center | Right | Right | Right |
| End | Tackle | Guard |  | Guard | Tackle | End |
| LE | LT | LG | C | RG | RT | RE |

Ball ●

(LHB), right halfback (RHB), and fullback (FB). Sometimes one of the HBs is used as a wide pass receiver and is called a flanker instead of halfback. This is often done by professional teams in the National Football League (NFL). In addition to a flanker, they also use a wide or split end (SE) and then refer to the other end, who isn't split, as the tight end (TE).

The most important position on any team is the quarterback. He is involved with every offensive play because he receives the snap from center and either hands off to another back, keeps the ball and runs with it, or drops back to throw a pass. He must be able to move quickly, he must have good hands to carefully control the ball, and he must be smart in order to remember what to do on every play. If he is a good runner, the coach will probably plan many running plays for him, and if he is a good passer, the team will usually throw a lot of passes in their offensive attack. This important position will be reviewed in much more detail elsewhere in this book.

The halfback position is most often filled by the best runner on the team. The best runner is not always the fastest runner, but he is one who is able to avoid tacklers by changing direction quickly. This is known as being "shifty," which simply means running to the left or right of a tackler to keep from being brought down. If the halfback is also fast, then he will be able to run around end and run away from tacklers. Halfbacks also must be able to catch passes and block for another back who may be carrying the ball.

The strongest and biggest back should be the fullback. The halfback usually runs around the defense, but the fullback is the back who, because of his size and power, runs through the line. He must be hard to tackle because of his strength and courage. If he is also a fast runner, he will be a valuable part of the team's offense because, if he gets through the line, he could run away from the rest of the defensive team. He must know how to catch short passes and must be a very good blocker to help the best runner, the halfback, to make long runs.

The flanker is often the best receiver on the team. He should also be a fast runner to allow him to run away from his defender and catch a

MAN-IN-MOTION PLAY. No. 44 runs parallel with the line of scrimmage until the ball is snapped; the offensive linemen display picture perfect form in their stances.

pass thrown by the QB. A good passer and a good flanker will give a team a quick way of scoring. The split end is a player with the same skills as a flanker. They must both be shifty in order to fake their defenders to keep them away from intercepting a pass. A pass completion is when the offensive team catches a pass; an interception is when the defensive team catches the offensive team's forward pass.

## DEFENSIVE TEAM

The eleven players who try to prevent the offensive team from scoring are known as the defensive team. Their job is to stop the offensive backs from running through the defensive linemen (or around them) and to stop the QB from completing passes to ends or backs. In order to do these things, the defense must use the special skills that their players must have to be successful. Let's review each defensive position and explain what the positions are and what the players must be able to do.

Defensive teams may use any number of players on the line (not like the offense where at least seven are required by the rules). Often the number of defensive linemen is based on one of the following: the formation the coach likes to use; or the best way to stop the offensive team;

SIX-MAN, EVEN DEFENSE. The six defensive linemen and two middle linebackers prepare to stop a twin left receiver offensive play.

or the abilities of the players on the defensive team. Although there are 3-, 4-, 7-, 8-, or 9-man lines used, the most common are the 5 and 6. More important, junior football leagues usually use the 6-man line but, because some also use the 5, both will be reviewed here. High school teams usually use both, too.

The most frequently used formations are the 6-2-3, 6-3-2, 5-3-3, and 5-4-2. The numbers after 6 and 5 refer to the position of the remaining players who are the defensive secondary or defensive backs. The 6-2-3, therefore, looks like this:

RDE   RDT        MG        LDT   LDE

SE          LT  LG    RG  RT  TE                          FL

QB

LH              FB

Both the 5- and 6-man lines have defensive ends (DE) and defensive tackles (DT), but they differ at the defensive guard position. In the 5-man line, there is only one guard. He is called the middle guard (MG) playing right in the middle of the defensive line opposite the offensive center. In the 6-man line, there are two guards—the left defensive guard (LDG) and right defensive guard (RDG). They play opposite the offensive guards.

The 5-man front arrangement of defensive linemen is shown above.

The DEs should be tall, quick, and strong to keep the offense from running around them. They must also be able to rush the passer. The DTs must be the biggest and strongest players on the team to keep the offense from running through the defense, and the DGs must be quick and strong to fight their way into the offensive line to throw their backs for a loss. There will be more on defensive formations and linemen in a later chapter.

The linebackers, as the name indicates, are the defensive backs who play just behind the defensive linemen. They usually make most of the tackles because they are very mobile and are difficult to block. They often move around behind their linemen to keep the offensive line-men from getting to them. The LBRs try to "plug" the holes in their defensive line, throw off the attempts to block them, and tackle the ball carrier as he tries to burst through the line. LBRs must also be prepared to drop back to protect against passes thrown in their area or zone of the field.

In the 6-2-3 there are two LBRs and in the 5-3-3 there are three. Many teams are currently using a 5-4-2 and a 4-4-3 where there are two inside linebackers called middle linebackers and two outside linebackers called cornerbacks.

Cornerbacks have to be faster than line-backers but must be just as good at tackling. They must make most of the tackles when the offense tries to run around end which brings the ball into cornerback country. They also have the difficult task of protecting against passes thrown to fast wide receivers such as split ends and flankers. In certain defensive plans, they cover areas of the field known as zones and must prevent offensive backs from trying to catch passes thrown in their defensive zones.

The last defensive section is the deep second-ary where the safeties play. In the 6-2-3, 5-3-3, and 4-4-3 there are three safeties called left, middle, and right safeties. However, in the 5-4-2 and 6-3-2 or other two-deep secondary align-

RCB      R        L        LCB
        MLB    MLB

**5-4 Front**

RCB     R              L       LCB
       MLB           MLB

**4-4 Front**

**3 Deep, 5-3-3**

**2 Deep, 5-4-2**

ments, there is a left safety and a right safety. Some of the various defensive formations and the position of the safeties often look like the diagram at the top of this page.

Safeties must be quick and alert players because they must rush in to help stop running plays or must react to the movements of pass receivers on pass plays. If they fail to do their job, in either instance, a touchdown may result.

They are the safeguard against the opponent's attempt to score; hence the name safety is applied to them.

The defensive unit must act together just as the offense does. To ensure their defensive plans are properly understood, a defensive huddle is called after every play. When the offensive team is in their huddle, the defense gathers on the other side of the line of scrimmage to decide

5-3 DEFENSE. The three linebackers are ready to fill the gaps between their five-linemen, odd-front defense.

OFFENSIVE VS DEFENSIVE FORMATIONS. Twin left wide receiver formation spreads the five-man defensive formation across the field.

which formation they want to use. The decision usually is based on the down, distance to make a first down or a touchdown, or many other factors. The defensive captain, often a linebacker, makes the decision, and every player must do his job to stop the offense.

Both offense and defense are fun to play. Some players prefer one more than the other; some like to play both ways. When possible, coaches should try to develop separate offensive and defensive units to achieve as much specialization as possible. This will allow more flexibility in developing skills and should result in each boy being assigned to a position he is most qualified for. A complete description of the physical skills required to play each position and the responsibilities of each position will be covered in the forthcoming chapters.

# 2

# The Quarterback

The most demanding position to play in football is that of quarterback. A boy must be an above average athlete to play this position. Coordination is an important talent in any sport; in order to be a good quarterback, an athlete must be able to completely control his legs, arms, and body.

The basic job of the QB is to call the play in the huddle, make sure he receives the snap from center, and then deliver (hand off) the ball quickly, surely, and with deception to the ball carrier. It is generally agreed by most coaches that a QB should be well built; he should be physically and mentally tough. Thin or heavy boys may be either too easily hurt or too slow to make the required agile moves in the backfield. Tall or short boys may either be too uncoordinated or not big enough to stand up under the body contact a QB often is exposed to. A good ball handler must be able to quickly

move his arms and hands as he turns, spins, and runs to meet the ball carrier at the hand-off place on each running play. He must have the same control over his legs and feet that a dancer has in order to make sure that he moves smoothly and gracefully in the backfield area on each play.

A QB should be able to run fast, be quick in his movements, and also be able to throw a forward pass accurately. A good passer can be developed by training and constant practice, if he doesn't have pure natural ability.

The correct form for passing begins with the stance. Balance is necessary in order to throw the ball well, so the boy must begin with his feet about a foot apart, pointing in the direction he wants to throw the ball. The ball should be brought up to his chest, the right hand (assuming he is right-handed) in throwing position on the ball while the left hand cradles the underside

QUARTERBACK POISED FOR THROW. The QB's throwing arm raises ball toward the back of his head while the other arm controls the ball.

QUARTERBACK PASS RELEASE. With ball cocked behind his head, QB steps toward target with his left leg, holding his left arm forward for balance.

QUARTERBACK THROWING TECHNIQUE. The ball is delivered over the top of the head and shoulder, pushing off the back leg while stepping toward the target.

QUARTERBACK PASS GRIP. QB places three fingers on the laces and forefinger near tip to prepare to throw.

of the ball. The left hand is also used to raise the ball to his chest and continue it upward until it is above the right ear. This places the ball in the launch position as the back leg (right leg) is set from which the body is projected forward. The forward step taken with the left leg must be directed at the target area the pass is to be thrown toward. The length of the stride with the left leg depends on the height of the boy but should usually be no longer than the width of his shoulders. A short stride usually causes the ball to be thrown too high; a long stride results in a low throw. Each boy must adjust his stride to the uniqueness of his body proportions.

A vital aspect of developing the skill of throwing a forward pass is the placement of the ball in the passer's hand. A review of many of the great passers indicates that each had his own special way of holding the ball. The key difference usually is based on the size of the passer's hand. A large hand can spread wide enough to place the index finger near the tip of the ball (but not on it) with the pinky and one or two other fingers on the laces. There are too many variations to cover but the basics must include an ability to grasp the ball rather than cradle it, a fingertip grip on the laces, and the index finger near the tip of the ball. If a spiral is not produced most of the time (say 8 out of 10 times), then the grip on the ball must be altered.

On rare occasions, the follow-through after the throw may be the problem. After the ball is thrown, the hand must continue through the passing arc in the same fashion as a baseball pitcher does when he throws the ball to the catcher. At the end of the delivery, the thumb is closer to the ground than the pinky, an indication that the hand turns counterclockwise after the ball is released.

It is also important to teach boys to throw hard. A pass thrown 10, 20, 30, or more yards may be thrown with equal velocity with only the trajectory angle adjusted to the longer distances. A sharply thrown pass will result in fewer interceptions and will enable the passer to better gauge his throwing angle to ensure getting the ball to where the receiver will be as he runs his pass pattern. A soft pass must be learned for short "dump" passes such as screen passes or other throws to backs slipping out of the backfield. They usually must be lofted to get them over the heads and arms of onrushing defensive linemen.

Another variable in quarterback technique is the placing of the hands under the center's backside. Some coaches prefer the left hand on top and the right hand under; others teach the opposite way. Regardless of hand placement, the back of the top hand must be pressed up against the center's rump, just under its downward curvature. The fingers must be spread wide with the heel of the other hand pressed up against the heel of the top hand with its fingers also spread wide. All ten fingers must be alert to capture the ball as the center brings it up hard to smack into the QB's hands. The ball is turned as it is brought up so that it fits into the QB's hands as he would grasp it in order to throw a pass. Coaches who advocate the right hand on top claim that the ball is ready for passing as soon as the QB gets the snap. The center must revolve the ball on the ground to get the laces down in order for them to be under the QB's right hand as he receives the snap. A similar advantage can be obtained for top left-handed QBs to get the laces to come up into the QB's under hand (right), so take your choice.

The QB should assume his stance behind the

QUARTERBACK PASS RELEASE. With eyes fixed on the receiver, the QB releases the ball at the top of the arc to obtain the required velocity and maximum accuracy.

QUARTERBACK–CENTER BALL EXCHANGE. The center snaps the ball into the QB's hands as he fires out to block the defensive lineman to his right.

QUARTERBACK AND RUNNING BACK STANCES. QB and RB are prepared to move when center snaps the ball to the quarterback.

center close enough to easily reach in with his hands but not so close as to cause him to squat by bending his knees too much. The knees should be very slightly bent and relaxed with both feet no wider than the QB's shoulders. The basic idea is to be comfortable and be ready to turn either way quickly without tripping or stumbling. Open-up steps or reverse pivots require complete leg and foot control. An open-up step is best illustrated by describing how the QB hands off to the FB on a straight ahead dive between the RG and RT. In this example, both backs must get to the hand-off area at the same time to ensure a smooth exchange.

The QB must push off his left foot and step toward his right with his right foot. The right foot should open up toward the right, quickly followed by the left foot stepping beyond the right foot. Open-up steps, therefore, are taken with the foot nearest the direction the QB is going toward.

Reverse pivots are made on the foot closest to the direction the QB wants to go to. In the same example as above, the QB should push off his left foot and turn 180 degrees on his right foot, spinning to his left toward the LH. After the left foot leaves the ground, it doesn't touch the ground again until it is pointed in the direction the QB is going toward—or almost to the same spot the right foot got to on the open-up step footwork above.

QUARTERBACK–RUNNING BACK APPROACH. QB turns away from the center to intersect with RB and hand-off the ball.

The advantage of the open-up technique is that the QB can get to the hand-off spot faster and can see the live action in front of him. The reverse pivot, although a fraction of a second slower, is more deceptive because it obscures the ball from the defense behind the QB's body. A good rule of thumb is: if the QB must come down the line of scrimmage (LOS), he should open up. If he is to release deeper in the backfield, he may use the reverse pivot. On I formation plays, where the FB and LH are set directly behind the QB, the reverse pivot easily permits the FB to run past the QB as the hand-off is made to the LH.

After either method, the QB must use deception to confuse the defense by not allowing them to see the ball or by making them think he still has the ball after he's handed it off to another back. He must realize that the defensive team's view of the ball is often obscured by the offensive linemen. In order to fake well, the QB must get as close as possible to the back he's handing off to, or faking to, without causing a collision between them. By getting close, he avoids holding the ball away from his body which would make it easier for the defense to see. When moving close to other backs, he must hold the ball in close to his belt and keep his elbows snug to his body.

A smooth moving QB must be able to move to his left or right with equal ability. This is best accomplished by quick, short steps with knees slightly bent and shoulders and head lowered as though he were running under the low branches of a tree. This coiled stature keeps the QB from standing erect which would cause his knees to lock and make it difficult for him to move quickly. A rigid, stiff-legged, upright stance increases the frequency of fumbles because any body contact between backs results in a shocking impact that may jar the ball loose. Contact often occurs because the QB and running back may not have their timing coordinated as they converge on the hand-off intersection. The QB must adjust his speed and extension of his arm to allow the running back to run at full speed, receive the ball, and not be jarred by contact with the QB. A good QB will focus his eyes on the ball carrier's belt and gently press the ball into his midsection with slight pressure into his body. If the center of the ball misses the center of the body, a fumble may result. QBs sometimes push the ball past the carrier's middle, causing it to go through and out the other side of his grasp. This can happen if the ball is tossed rather than pressed into the carrier's body or if the QB is holding the ball near the point instead of in the middle of the ball.

Coaches must plan on a great deal of practice on hand-offs between QBs and running backs. This must be done at every practice session and prior to every game. This activity must also include pitches from the QB to backs running end sweeps. The QB uses the reverse pivot, pulls the ball away from the center, and in one continuous motion tosses the ball underhanded in front of the sweeping runner. This permits the ball carrier to run at full speed and receive the ball in stride as he races around end.

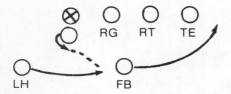

A great deal of discipline must be enforced on the specific techniques the QB must perform because he is the main gear of the offensive mechanism. The coach must be mindful of spending an equal amount of time practicing hand-offs and pitches to the left and to the right. By developing all the skills of his trade, a young QB can get many years of experience as he progresses to and through high school. If he learns improper methods, his team and career will suffer. Be attentive to him.

QUARTERBACK HAND-OFF. With both hands on the rear half of the ball, the QB extends the ball into the RB's midsection while ensuring that their bodies do not make contact.

# 3

# The Running Backs

## HALFBACK

Running backs are expected to carry the ball through or around the defense. Halfbacks are usually the outside runners who must also run inside when required. In order to be effective as a halfback, a boy must be a fast runner and have a relatively strong body to withstand the impact of frequent tackling. However, it is not sufficient to just be fast, because a good runner must be able to adjust his speed to different situations. A ball carrier must be able to change his direction quickly to avoid tacklers. To do this, he must run "under control," because if he runs at full speed among tacklers, it will be difficult to be shifty and elusive. Halfbacks, therefore, must learn to run at less than full out when they are changing course and to accelerate when they see "daylight."

A coach must review each running back's technique to help him learn when and where to adjust his speed. For example, if a HB is going full steam on an end sweep, he may not be able to cut upfield toward the goal line if he spots an opening in the defensive pursuit. This is also true when a play calls for the QB to pitch a lateral to the HB at the start of a sweep. Running at full speed increases the chance of a fumble by the HB when he tries to catch the toss. However, if he is to receive a hand-off from the QB on a quick play into the line, the chance of a fumble is small and he can take off as fast as he can. This is very important because the sooner he gets to the blocking area, the better chance he has at making it through and across the LOS for a gain. Blocking linemen often have difficulty sustaining their blocks and a slow-moving back may get to the LOS just as the defensive man recovers from the blocker's charge to make the tackle.

In order to run well at the start of each play, the backs must learn a proper stance. They must

RUNNING BACK TURNING UPFIELD. The running back must plant his turning foot as he whips his outside leg upfield to make the turn at maximum speed.

forward on the right fingers, but the left foot must relieve some of the pressure to avoid having the right hand bear some of the weight. The coach should pull the right arm out to see if the stance has placed the weight evenly on both feet. If the back falls forward when this is done, the stance must be adjusted. At every practice session a good coach will observe stances and starting steps to ensure correct execution.

The starting steps are easily taken in all directions from this stance. If the run must go right, the feet should turn right as the right foot is raised for a short first step. The left leg will quickly swing out of the stance for a longer second step as it crosses over the right. A run to the left is exactly opposite with the left foot making the short first step and the right crossing over. Both arms must be used to swing the body quickly in the desired direction and then go directly into their short pumping strokes to quicken the running speed. On runs straight ahead, the first step should be with the left foot with a driving thrust off the back (right) leg. A diagonal, slanting run toward the right requires the first step to be made with the right foot and an opposite slant to the left starts with the left. Again, the arms should help turn the body and start churning to gain speed. Track coaches teach their sprinters to control the stroke length of their arms because legs move in time with their opposite arms. If arms are slow moving and dangle in an uncontrolled manner, a boy will be a slow runner. The best runners look like poetry in motion, their arms and legs moving in a disciplined rhythm.

It is strongly recommended that all players, particularly backs, be timed with a stopwatch. The general procedure in football is to time each boy in a 40-yard sprint. Some coaches time 100 yards and 10 yards to determine long- and short-range speed, but 40 yards is more representative of a distance a boy may be required to run in a game. Have him start from his best stance and start the clock as his hand lifts off the ground. By timing players frequently, a coach can monitor improvement. If no reduction occurs, some corrective measures must be taken, particularly with young boys just beginning to learn how to start and run. By developing a boy's thighs, a coach can help him

be able to run laterally toward the sideline, diagonally toward either end, or straight ahead into the line. A stance must be able to provide a launching pad to go in all directions without letting the defense determine where the back is going. A flaw in a back's stance may "tip off" when he is going forward or sideward.

A good stance starts with the placement of the feet. If the back is right-handed, his right foot must be slightly further away from the LOS than his left. A good rule is to position the front of the right foot parallel with the instep (laces) of the left foot. The feet should be as wide as the shoulders, pointing straight ahead. The back must now squat, placing the left elbow on the top of the left thigh, with the hand hanging downward. The tips of the right hand must barely touch the ground with the right arm extending straight down from the right shoulder. By raising the rump to a height that will make the back parallel with the ground, the heel of the right foot will come an inch or so off the ground. This will also tend to lean the body

RUNNING BACK START-UP. RB quickly sprints toward line of scrimmage as QB moves toward him with the ball.

run faster because running is nothing more than the raising and lowering of legs. Strong thigh muscles will enable a boy to do this more quickly and thereby run faster. Drills and calisthenics that will help build strong legs, thighs, and bodies will be described in Chapter 9. Other drills that will teach players how to perform specific actions will be covered throughout the text to further explain training techniques.

Learning how to run in traffic and to change direction sharply is another skill that good running backs must develop. To help train HBs, a coach should take time in each practice session to have the boys perform a variety of running drills. For example, place a number of objects (pylons, dummies, old tires, etc.) in a straight row about two yards apart and have the players run a zig-zag course through them as follows:

OPEN FIELD RUNNING. The ball carrier hurdles a tackler while raising his leg and arm for balance and ball control to ensure maximum speed.

Have them run as fast as they can, staying as close to the dummies as possible, shifting the ball from one arm to the other as they run around each dummy, and hand the ball off to the player waiting at the front of the opposite line of players. The main objective is to have them learn how to control their bodies in high speed–sharp turn situations. They will find that if they run too fast, they will not be able to turn (cut) sharply and will drift far away from the desired running lane. It will also allow them to learn what their body control will produce, and they and the coach will be able to determine what their weaknesses are. Some boys run with long strides; this results in a slow pace and an inability to get the feet in the right place at the turning points. A series of quick, short steps is the best technique along with something called "body lean." This means running around corners with the feet going wide enough to circle the end of the dummies but letting the body lean over each dummy as it is passed. This skill helps keep the body away from a tackler. It is comparable to taking a turn in a car on two wheels but with the lean in the opposite direction.

A variation of the drill can be used by having the backs run over the first two dummies and then around the remaining ones. This not only gets the backs used to getting their legs up high while running fast but also forces them to stop suddenly in order to run around the third dummy as they change direction to make the turn. It is also a good drill to have them run over all the dummies at full speed. This will help build the valuable thigh muscles, so important in improving running speed.

Next, stand the dummies up (or have them held upright) in staggered, opposite rows and have the backs run through them like this:

As they approach each dummy, they must shift the ball away from the dummy, straight-arm the dummy, and run as fast as they can with body lean away from the dummy as they would try to avoid a tackler. The straight-arm technique is used to ward off a would-be tackler by extending the free arm straight out from the shoulder as the player pushes the tackler away with his hand. A strong straight-arm done in conjunction with a lean away from the tackler on a sharp cut will usually allow a ball carrier to avoid being tackled.

These are only a few drills intended to teach body control and develop special skills for running backs. Running activity of all kinds—starting from a good stance, coupled with disciplined arm and leg movements—will help backs improve their ball-carrying ability. The specific technique of holding the ball, shifting it from arm to arm, and protecting it from being fumbled will be covered in the fullback review that follows.

QUARTERBACK SCRAMBLING. The QB uses his straight-arm to avoid a tackler in order to throw a pass.

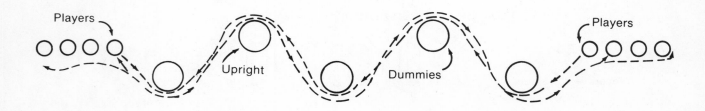

## FULLBACK

Most of what was highlighted for HBs also applies to fullbacks (FBs). All of the running requirements and the stance techniques are identical. The basic difference between the positions is in the role each is expected to play in the offensive scheme. Whereas the HB is called upon for speed and primarily outside running, the FB is expected to be strong, not necessarily as fast, and usually is an inside runner. Most football coaches look for a bull who is not slow and is eager to run over and through tacklers. He is not required to be shifty, but if he has that talent he'll find occasions to use it. He is expected to be hard to tackle and to be strong enough to bowl over a defensive player to gain a few yards for a first down. His running style must be geared to the basic role the team depends on him for. That means he must learn to run low, close to the ground, and with a decided forward lean. By running low he will not expose too much of his body to the tacklers' hands. Staying close to the ground will enable him to get under the defensive charge of opposing linemen, to straighten them up as he runs into and through them. The forward lean is intended to allow him to fall forward when he is tackled to get maximum yardage out of every running play.

The FB is often asked to get the "tough" yards, when one or two yards are needed for a first down or a touchdown and everyone at the game knows he is going to get the ball. To gain yards in these tight situations, he must start quickly from his balanced stance, accelerate as much as he can, receive the ball from the QB, and turn on all the power he can to burst through the mass of arms, legs, and bodies. Because FBs are usually heavier, their starting speed is normally slower than HBs. This can be compensated for by having them "cheat" up closer to the LOS than the HB's starting set position. The term "cheat" means that a back should adjust his set position on certain plays to gain a specific advantage. If the backs regularly line up (set) four yards behind the LOS, the FB can cheat up a few inches to enable him to get quickly to the designated "hole" or place in the offensive line where the blocking will give him

some daylight to run through. Cheating is also used to achieve the proper timing on a wide variety of plays when the QB and the HB or FB are not intersecting effectively. The coach must be alert to the situations that may require this technique.

Because the FB is closer to the LOS, less than a few seconds elapse when he reaches the defensive front line. In that time, he must securely obtain and tuck away the ball to avoid fumbling it when the impact of the tackle jolts his body. This exchange between QB and running back is one of the most vital coaching areas in football. The QB's task has already been covered in Chapter 2. The running back's effort is simple but critical. As he runs toward the hole, his eyes must focus on the execution of the offensive linemen to determine how successful they are in blocking the defense. His eyes must not be on the QB, but his peripheral vision will make him aware of the QB's location as they approach each other at the hand-off intersection. The ball carrier must raise the arm closest to the QB so that his elbow is about one foot away from his rib cage and his forearm is parallel with his chest. The other arm's elbow is about four inches away from his belt, and its forearm extends toward the QB on a plane even with his belt.

The basic design of the receiving technique is to create a trap for the ball to be captured in. By raising the elbow nearest the QB, the back provides an accessible opening for the ball. The other arm is used as the bottom and opposite wall of the "basket." If the QB extends the ball too far into the area, the biceps of the other arm should not allow it to slip through and out of his grasp. The distance between the two forearms should be a few inches wider than the diameter of the ball. As soon as the ball is pressed into his diaphragm area, the ball carrier must clamp on the ball from above and below. As the forearms move toward the ball, both hands must seek the ball with fingers spread wide. There must not be any stiffness or rigidity in arms, wrists, hands, or fingers as this will impact the football and increase the chance of a fumble.

Most coaches advise backs to hold their hands on both ends of the football while they're

QUARTERBACK–RUNNING BACK HANDOFF. RB raises nearest elbow to the quarterback to receive the ball as QB prepares to press the ball into the RB's midsection.

running in traffic through the line. This is added insurance against a fumble but, because it restricts running speed, the ball carrier should move the ball under one arm as soon as he is out of the crowd at the LOS. This final movement of the ball can be a two-handed action which should move one of the ball's points up into an armpit while the fingers spread over the other point and firmly press the ball up into the armpit. It is wise to hold the ball with the arm farthest away from the nearest tackler. This will permit the other arm to straight-arm the tackler while the ball is protected away from him.

Defensive coaches instruct their players to try to pull the ball carrier's hands off the ball or his elbows away from his body. Either of these techniques can cause a fumble. Therefore, the offensive coach should closely observe the manner in which his players hold the ball. A good drill to teach the backs how to hang on to the ball is easily set up. Have some of your linemen kneel down alongside each other in a row. Form another row opposite from them. Leave a lane a yard wide for the backs to run through. Have the QB hand off to each back (starting from a good stance) and tell the back

to run down the lane with the ball held on both ends. The linemen must try to strip him of the ball by pulling on his hands, fingers, and elbows. If the back makes it through the entire row without fumbling, he must try to bowl over the dummy held erect by another lineman at the end of the lane. The back then goes back and gets on the end of line to await another turn. After a dozen run-throughs, have the backs run in the opposite direction to permit the linemen to use their opposite hands for the attack on the ball. In addition, tell the back to move the ball under one arm when he gets to the end of the row and straight-arm the dummy as he would a defensive back in a ball game. Much later in the season, the above drill can be executed with backs holding the ball under one arm going through the lane to let them realize the strength

they will need if that situation should ever arise in a game. It's good practice for the linemen, too, to teach them how to cause a fumble.

Many descriptions of great running backs include a reference to a "high-stepping" style of running. For decades coaches tried to teach their backs to run with knees raised high in each stride. This is a great way to develop strong thigh muscles to increase overall speed but many coaches now believe the high-knee technique is not as effective as it was supposed to be. Instead, they are teaching a low foot-raise style for a surefooted, stronger controlled form of running. It is often referred to as a *glide* made famous by the great Jimmy Brown, probably the best running back in history. Larry Csonka, of more recent vintage, has also perfected a similar running style wherein his feet

RUNNING BACK BALL CONTROL. The running back circles left end with the ball in his left arm, forefinger over the point of the ball; right arm is free to straight-arm pursuit.

hardly come off the ground more than a few inches. The above "fumbling" drill can also be used to practice the glide. In this application, the kneeling linemen must be instructed to try to grab the runner's feet, ankles, or shins. When this is first attempted, most backs will trip and fall forward, but later they will become more accustomed to the demands on their leg and foot strength and will develop better balance and stability. With this ability, a ball carrier can become more effective with his forward lean and low-profile running through the traffic at the LOS. These are the skills a good fullback must bring into a game.

# 4

# The Wide Receivers

## FLANKER/SPLIT END

The primary function of these positions is to catch passes. In order to catch passes, a wide receiver (WR) must be able to get away from defenders and to catch the football. Each of these requirements have many coachable areas that must be reviewed.

Catching a football requires strong fingers and hands, good reflexes and coordination, proper technique, and plenty of practice. A great deal of concentration is necessary to catch the ball because there are many things that must be done in order to be successful most of the time.

The search for players who can be receivers should begin with a throwing and catching session. Take the QB prospects and have them throw to aspiring receivers about 10 to 15 yards away. Arrange the players like this:

After a QB throws to a receiver, the receiver catches the ball, tosses it to the QB standing alongside him, and then moves to the back of the line. The coach must instruct the boys to:

1. Follow the flight of the ball all the way until it hits their fingers.

2. Catch the ball with their thumbs pointing inward when the ball is thrown chest high or above.

3. Catch the ball with thumbs pointing outward on throws below the chest.

4. Catch the ball with the heels of the hands opening to accept the ball when throws are off to one side or the other.

5. Allow the fingers to be relaxed, not stiff and rigid, when the ball reaches them.

6. Pull the ball in the direction of its flight and tuck it into the safety of the receiver's arms as soon as possible to avoid dropping or fumbling it; try not to stop the ball abruptly when it hits the fingers and hands because the ball will often pop out from the impact.

Perhaps the most important of all and worthy of repeating is the old axiom: "watch the ball into your hands." Many passes are dropped because the receiver takes his eyes off the ball at the last second. By telling him to see it hit his fingers, you'll be urging him to follow it all the way.

The next drill to employ is the basic pass route throwing drill. Arrange two lines of receivers with QBs between them to take turns throwing the ball.

Have the receivers run only square-ins and sideline patterns. This requires them to test their ability to run and catch at the same time while executing the most frequently used pass patterns. When a receiver runs a pass pattern from one line, he returns to the other line to give him practice catching from the left and right sides of the field. The coach must observe each boy's

performance and be prepared to recommend corrective action. One of the most common failings is for a receiver to raise his arms too early while running a pattern. This will affect his coordination and prevent him from running properly. The rule to follow is to "only raise your arms when the ball arrives." Another thing to look for is the activity after a pass is caught. Teach the boys to turn upfield and run at least 5 to 10 yards at full speed after safely putting the ball away. This must become a reflex action to be repeated after every reception in practice to make it automatic in a game.

After thoroughly evaluating each boy, the coach must decide which are the most capable and qualified to go into more intensified training. This will involve learning many other pass patterns and becoming very familiar with the wide variety of defenses used to stop a passing attack. Wide receivers are a valuable part of an offense's attacking strength. They perform a function that must be performed well if a team is to be successful.

In order to consistently get away from defensive backs, a WR must have better than average speed; he must have elusive moves while running pass patterns; and he must be able to read defensive coverage to know how to adjust his pass routes. A pass pattern is a designed route a WR must run to coordinate a pass play with the QB. If the QB knows where the WR is going to run, he will be able to anticipate the WR's path and throw the ball to him before a defender can knock down or intercept the pass.

A pass pattern begins with a good stance. A WR should use the same stance used by the running backs but can lean farther forward because WRs never have to run parallel to the LOS as the backs do. By leaning forward and putting their rear foot a few inches farther back, they can explode forward when the ball is

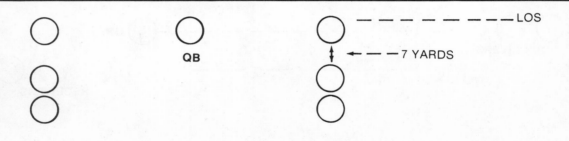

QUARTERBACK LOOKS FOR A RECEIVER. Standing in the pocket with the ball poised for delivery, the QB scans the secondary for an open receiver.

snapped and sprint down the field. However, running good pass routes does not always require speed. For example, a sideline pattern will succeed if the WR creates the illusion that he's running straight downfield and suddenly cuts sharply at a 90-degree angle and races for the sideline. If he is running at full speed coming off the LOS, he will not be able to make the sharp cut necessary to get away from the safety covering him. Each receiver must develop his own style based on his speed and ability to make the sharp cut. Regardless of technique, the WR must remember to always make his turn by pushing off the foot farthest from the direction of his turn. A sideline pattern to the right would require the kind of footwork shown below. Some coaches teach the WR to move his head as he makes his turn to add to the impression that he is going to continue straight ahead. This technique is called "throwing your head." It is not recommended for young players because it gives them something else to think about that

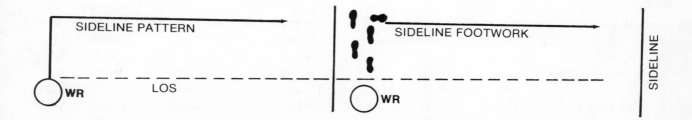

isn't as important as cutting properly (sharply) and catching the ball. Another activity that falls in the same category is a foot-dragging style that some coaches feel can help the WR make a sharper turn. In the above sideline pattern, the foot drag would be done with the last step taken by the right foot before the turning step. It is intended to help the WR throw on the brakes to help him turn more quickly. Here again, it is an unnecessary technique for youngsters and is better applied at college and professional levels. Coaches should observe each WR's stance, release, and cutting ability at each practice session and work with him to correct any deficiencies.

The various pass routes place different demands on the WR. The "hook" pattern requires more speed than the sideline because the WR is trying to make the defender think he's running a fly pattern. When he gets the defender backpedaling downfield, he stops abruptly on his outside (nearest the sideline) leg and "hooks" in to catch the ball. If the ball has not yet arrived, he must start coming back toward the QB to widen the distance between the defender and the ultimate arrival of the ball. Receivers must be cautioned not to try to start running with the pass until they actually catch it. This is particularly true on a hook pass because the WR expects the defender to tackle him from behind when his back is turned. This anxiety is often referred to as "hearing footsteps" and is a frequent cause of dropped passes. Pass receivers must be taught to catch the ball because they're going to be tackled whether they catch the ball or not, so they might just as well have something to show for their effort.

The "fly" pattern requires little in the way of turning but does require a great deal of speed. However, because all other pass patterns shouldn't start with full speed, neither should the fly. A receiver must try to start all patterns in the same manner to avoid allowing the defenders to detect any "tip-offs" to where the pass is going. In the fly pattern, the WR must try to get the defender to depart from the usual backpedal coverage and get him to turn and run with him. Whenever a receiver can get the defender to turn, an advantage is gained. Look at the flag and post patterns. They begin just like the fly pattern. If the defender turns toward the sideline, the fly pattern will be successful.

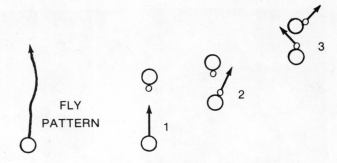

**THE THREE PARTS OF THE FLY**

In order to make this happen, the WR should steer his course slightly outward (No. 2) to allow the defender to assume that a flag pattern is being run. The post and flag patterns are opposites. As in the fly, the WR must try to get the defender to turn the wrong way. This can best be illustrated by reviewing the footsteps taken at the important turn area in each pattern.

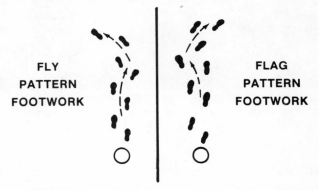

When defenders play up close or "tight" to a WR, the above footwork may be successful. However, when a safety plays back (or "off") a WR, the technique may be a waste of time. Instead, the WR should draw on his reserve of speed and turn on full steam to run away from his defender. In addition, the WR should sharpen his route angle to get farther away from the safety. When he does this, however, he must be careful not to run into another defender's zone or an interception may result.

Defensive pass coverage may be man-to-man or zone, or a combination of both. Man-to-man, or "man" coverage as it is often referred to, assigns a defensive back to cover each receiver wherever he may run his pass pattern.

In zone coverage, each defensive back is assigned a zone or area of the field to protect. Any receiver(s) in his zone must be covered by the zone defender.

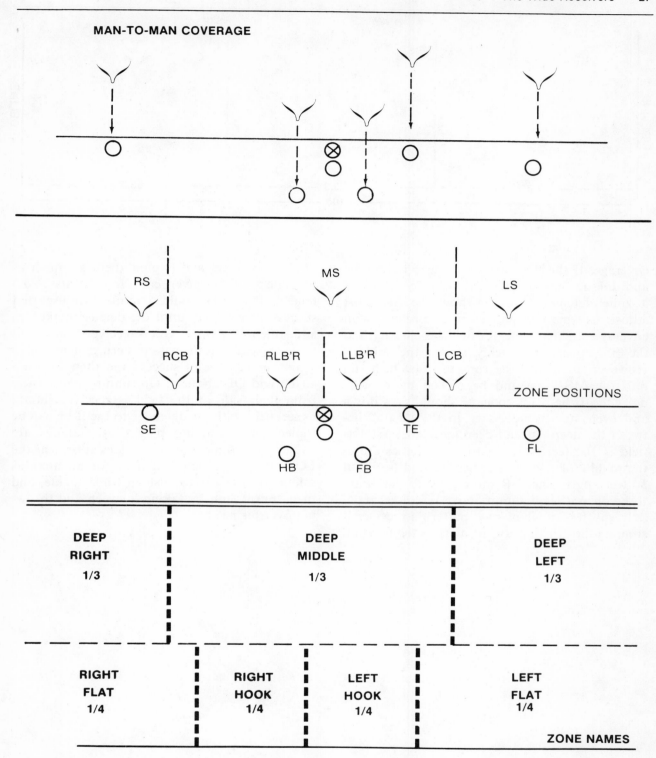

**MAN-TO-MAN COVERAGE**

ZONE POSITIONS

ZONE NAMES

A combination of both coverages may be used particularly if a WR is a very dangerous offensive weapon. In such instances, a defender may be assigned to give him man coverage while the remaining defensive secondary plays a zone. Many variations of all three coverages may be used and a WR must learn how to determine what the defense is using. A good technique to use to make this determination is the square pattern. If the SE runs at his defender and then runs a square-in toward the middle of the field, and if the RS follows him, he may be in a man

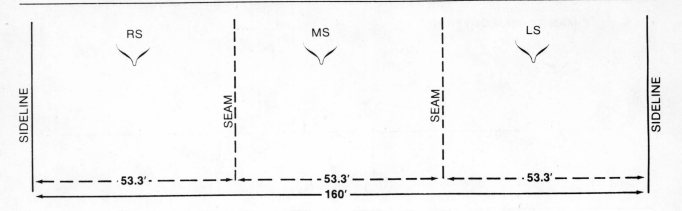

coverage. If the RS stays in his deep right zone and doesn't follow the SE, they are probably in a zone defense. Consider how the SE must adjust his square-in pattern in accordance with coverage. In man, the RS will be chasing and the SE must run quickly across the middle. However, in zone if he runs too fast he'll run into the MS zone and be picked up by that defender. If he reads zone, he should slow down and even stop if necessary in the "seam" between the deep left and deep middle zones. The field is 160 feet wide, and if the safeties are in the middle of their zones, they should be about 50 feet apart. The WR must get into that seam to be open. (See diagram above.)

Regardless of which pass pattern a receiver is running, he must always be alert to the location of the defenders and exploit them as much as possible. If a receiver constantly beats a defender, the QB should continue to use that successful pass play until the defense makes an adjustment to stop it. Good receivers must continue to search for a pass pattern that promises a high percentage of success and then tell their coach and QB about it. On running plays away from their side of the field, a receiver should experiment with his defender to see if he can be fooled on a running play pass. Safeties are counted on to make many tackles at or near the LOS. A wise coach will look for an anxious safety who yearns to rush in for a tackle, and then "burn" him by faking a sweep and throwing over his head.

# 5

# The Offensive Linemen

## TIGHT END

A tight end is often referred to as a fast tackle who can catch a football. The reference recognizes that a TE must be as big or nearly as big as a tackle but must be quicker in order to get involved in the team's passing attack. A TE must be big because he is a vital member of the front wall that must block defensive linemen on running plays. In particular, the TE is usually face to face with the biggest, toughest defensive lineman, the strongside left tackle. For that reason, the TE should be a competent blocker and be mentally tough to withstand the rigors of a hard encounter.

A coach should begin his hunt for a TE by racing all the big linemen against a time clock and then against each other. This will identify the speed of each candidate. Next, a pass catching drill (see Chapter 4) should be held to assess their ability to catch. By comparing the results of both evaluations, the coach should select the players who rank the highest in each category and prepare them for more intensive training.

The first phase of TE training should start with blocking. A fast, pass catching TE who can't block well cannot help an offense be successful. Primary requirements for good blocking are strength and quickness. In order to develop these, many drills can be put to use. They are covered in depth in a later chapter and can be used to prepare all offensive linemen in the skills of blocking. Blocking instructions also are covered later. After blocking skills are taught, a third measurement of a TE's value can be rated by a coach. The players who rank highest should be the team's tight ends.

In some offensive formations, the TE is directed to assume a position either to the right side next to the right tackle or to the left side next to the left tackle. In a one TE formation, the other end is the split end who is also re-

DOUBLE TIGHT END, WIDE FLANKER OFFENSE. This power oriented offense is set to block a 4-3 defense.

quired to split to either side, opposite to the TE. There are other formations that use two tight ends, and a few others use two split ends and no TEs. If a coach is more pass oriented, he may be inclined to use a one or two split-end offense. Coaches who prefer to run the ball will usually use two tight ends and throw the ball only as a surprise weapon. The decision as to what type offense to use can be based on the abilities of the players, usually the QB's ability to throw or the running back's ability to run. However, the availability of good wide receivers or tight ends can help shape a coach's decision, too.

## OFFENSIVE TACKLES

An offensive tackle (OT) must be the biggest and strongest player on the team. His primary skill must be blocking because he is the man who must neutralize equally big defensive linemen. Without a good tackle, a running game will be hard to come by.

Usually big players are slow, but slowness can be worked on by a diligent coach. In order to get an advantage on the defensive player, a tackle must be quick. Quickness can be achieved through the use of agility and reaction drills.

Whereas all players must participate in such drills, they are particularly vital to the bigger offensive and defensive linemen. There are dozens of techniques that can be used to quicken the slowness of young players; some are covered in Chapter 9.

Equally important for the success of a running attack is the development of sound blocking skills. Size and strength alone will not guarantee good results, so a wise coach will use most of the time spent with offensive linemen in sharpening their blocking ability.

Once again we must begin with a good stance. Taller players have to adjust their basic stance by moving their back foot a little further back than the shorter players. The basics include good balance by keeping the feet as wide as the shoulders, the weight evenly spread on both feet, and the forward extended arm and the back parallel to the ground. The rear foot must be poised in a launch position with the heel raised off the ground to allow the weight to be centered on the pad just behind the toes.

The head and neck are vital to the blocking scheme. Raise the head slightly to bring the eyes in focus with the opponent's numerals and bow the neck in anticipation of the strength it must expend upon contact. Coaches of young players

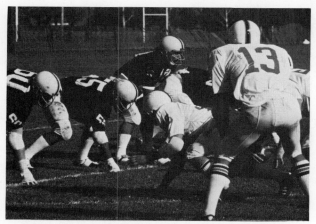

OFFENSIVE LINEMEN'S STANCE. Right guard and right tackle (dark jerseys) are set, waiting for ball to be snapped.

do not advise the use of head and neck as a thrusting weapon into the opponent. Rather, they teach that contact should be made with the shoulder, supported by a raised forearm strengthened by holding the hand tightly up against the chest.

The "shield" formed by shoulder and arm must be driven by the body and legs into the defender, with three basic adjustments depending on which area the ball carrier will be running into. For example, if the ball is going to the "hole" on the left side of a right tackle, like this . . .

. . . he would have to drive across the defender's chest and get his head on the defensive tackle's (DT) inside in order to have the shield force the DT away from the ball carrier. As the head and neck reach their desired location, they should turn the DT's body while the legs and body extend their force to overcome the defender. The exact opposite technique is used when a defender must be blocked in the other direction, such as a LT would be faced with on the same play run to the other side of the center.

The third rushing block is the "no penetration" type which, as the name implies, is de-

signed to keep the defender from driving through the offensive tackle and into the backfield. This can be accomplished in a few ways but the most common are drive or crab blocks. A drive or fire block requires the OT to start quickly on the snap sound to gain the advantage of having his momentum overwhelm the DT's strength while the shoulder and forearm come up through the DT's chest. This upward drive is intended to straighten up the opponent to take away his forward charge.

The other nonturning block is the crab block which can be very effective when alternated with the drive or fire. The OT must turn his body and whip his hip into the defender while his hands and feet, on all four, attempt to entrap and confine the opponent to the LOS. These blocks are particularly effective on plays running outside the interior line area when backfield action requires a few seconds to get outside. If a defensive lineman were to penetrate the offensive line, he would likely cause a loss of yardage, so it is vital that line blocking prevent that from happening.

Another application is on a quick pass play such as a short pass to the tight end just over the defensive linemen's heads. When blockers show a pass block technique, linebackers quickly retreat to cover their zone areas. To deceive them and prevent that from occurring, have the OT and OG fire out; that will make the linebackers think that a running play is coming and the pass should find them out of position. It is usually more effective when a play-action fake is used to further indicate a running play.

A play-action pass play is one which to all observers appears to begin as a running play but ends up as a pass play. The most common is the "fake dive, pass" which looks like this . . .

. . . when the QB fakes a hand-off to the running back while the linemen fire out at their nearest defensive linemen. The LLB comes up to make the apparent tackle only to find that the TE has slipped in behind him to catch the quick pass from the QB. Because offensive interior linemen are not allowed beyond the LOS, they cannot fire out at a linebacker and must confine themselves to an opponent on the LOS.

Pass-blocking technique for the OT will be covered in the blocking requirements for the offensive guards (OG) in the next segment. Other blocking will be covered in Chapter 10.

## OFFENSIVE GUARD

The OG must be a player possessing a wide range of talent. He must be strong enough to block powerful defensive linemen, quick enough to seek out and block big linebackers, and agile enough to pull out of the line and into his own backfield to either lead the ball carrier around end or to trap out on an unsuspecting DT or DE.

The interior blocking skills are the same as those required for the OT. When defenses feature defensive guards (DG) as seen in the 4- and 6-man lines, the OG has an opponent right on his nose and must be able to block him left or right. His drive block and crab block are frequently used, but in the 5-man defenses, he usually has to deal with the superstar of the defense—the linebacker.

Blocking the LBR presents an assortment of problems. If the offensive backfield is deceptive and confusing to the LBR, he may be momentarily frozen in his area; this will enable the OG to reach him and block him out of the play. If there is no difficulty "reading" the offense, the LBR will quickly react and make the OG's attempt a futile one. When a quick dive is run right through an OG, he has to take the LBR whichever way is easiest for him. Linebackers are taught to step up into the hole and meet the OG with an upward shoulder and forearm shiver in an attempt to straighten him up and nullify his blocking strength.

For that reason, the OG must stay low and drive into and up through the LBR to force him backward and overcome his power. It is one of the classic struggles in football and a quick-starting, hard-driving, strong OG can make an

offense go just by handling the all-important linebacker.

The down block on the middle guard (MG) in the 5-man line and the out block on the DT are other techniques frequently used by the OG. These can be double-team or one-on-one blocks. A double-team is when two offensive players block one defender as in the diagrams below:

Usually a coach will ask for a double-team when a defender is too big, strong, or quick for one offensive player to block by himself. It tends to ensure that one key defender will definitely be out of the way on that play. On such a block, the offensive linemen must equalize the load by attempting to share the blocking surface of the opponent. As seen above, the OG must drive his near shoulder and forearm into the side of the opponent to add his force and strength to his teammate's block and overpower his man. The uncovered offensive man in both cases is the OG; he must take his lead step toward his teammate and then drive into the opponent. This is intended to safeguard against the defender's quick penetration between the blocking pair against him. The rule is: don't fire at him because when you get there diagonally, he most likely will not still be there; rather, anticipate his forward movement and head him off by getting there first.

The pull and trap blocking requires a balanced stance that can be used to launch from either the OG's left or right. Use the near arm to the desired direction as a swinging device and quickly turn and step with the lead leg, which is also the one nearest to the direction in which the OG is going. Once underway, he must stay low and under control until he sees and approaches the man he is to block. The element of surprise is a key to success, and the OG must be quick and decisive in his execution.

One of the typical trap blocks is the out-block on a DE.

The backs are flying out of their starting positions in their eagerness to get through the hole. The OG has to beat them to the hole area and get the DE out of their way. If he can, he should try to drive through him, getting his head on the hole-side of the defender to ensure that he doesn't charge back into the hole. There are many times when the DE is wary of this trap and he doesn't come too far across the LOS, thereby making it difficult for the OG to move him out of the running lane. When that happens, the OG may elect to throw a cross-body block in an attempt to prevent the DE from getting the runner.

A cross-body block is similar to the crab block except it comes off a running start. The basic approach is to whip the hips and legs in a swinging motion to cause the hips and body weight to make contact with the defender's thighs and mid-body area. In order to be successful, the block must be thrown at short range to ensure contact and impact. If started too far away, the defender can usually ward off or dodge the attack. Upon impact, a rolling action will sustain the contact and increase the chances of success.

Pass blocking is the most vital skill a pass-oriented team has to depend on. A good passer with standout receivers can produce little yardage or points if they don't have time to execute. Effective pass blocking can provide the time required to exploit the defensive pass coverage and lead to explosive, crowd- and player-pleasing results.

The pass blocker's basic position must appear to be similar to an ape's posture. As soon as an

QUARTERBACK POCKET PASS. The QB sets up seven yards deep, directly behind the center as pass blockers give him time to throw.

OG or OT comes out of his stance by taking a backward step with the leg farthest from the center, he must assume a semicrouch stance with knees flexed, arms hanging loosely at his side, and body coiled and ready to spring. He must then bring his hands up to his chest with fists clenched to be ready to counter the defender's charge. When he gets close enough to fire into, the pass blocker must rise out of his crouch and drive up and through the opponent's chest to alter his stride and break his power base. No sooner has he done this than he must shuffle quickly back into position and crouch in preparation to strike out again as the defender rushes over toward the QB.

A good guideline to follow is to have the blocker use his back as a camera, always focused on the QB. This conveys the thought that he must try to be aware of the QB's location to enable him to adjust his movements to protect the passes. A common error that must be overcome is the loss of control of the blocker's balance. He must not attempt to thrust from long distance, but should get up close to the opponent before exploding from his crouch. Also important is the quick recovery from the explosion in order to shuffle back into attack position.

The spread of the blocker's feet is also vital to his balance. If he allows his feet to get less than shoulder width apart, the defender's "swim" technique will force the blocker to lose his balance and be beaten. The swim motion is the swinging of the arms frequently used by competent pass rushers to deliver a blow to the head or shoulders of a blocker to get him out of the way.

If your offense is going to depend on the passing game, you would be wise to practice pass blocking as often as possible to develop this important skill. A variety of special drills can be used to teach the proper techniques. For example, by setting up designated areas with dummies, pylons, etc., a series of drills can be implemented.

Dummies 1 and 2 are used as boundaries to simulate adjoining linemen. On the coach's signal, the rusher tries to charge through the blocker to reach Dummy 3 (the QB) set at a seven-yard-deep location from where a QB usu-

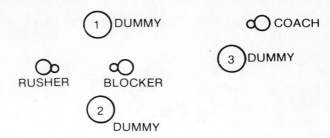

ally throws. The blocker may react to the rusher's change in direction and should try to make at least three "hits" before the coach's whistle blows. This would represent enough time for the QB to get the throw off to a receiver. A slight variation is to have two hits and a "chop." A chop is in reality a crab or cross-body block that is designed to take the defender off his feet or at least to ensnare him in the blocker's body. It is an important part of an artful pass blocker's repertoire.

Another effective drill is to line two defenders on either side of a blocker.

On the coach's signal, one rusher attacks the blocker while the other runs away from him or hesitates and crosses around behind his teammate's path. This is one of a variety of "stunts" that can be attempted to see if the blocker can react and adjust to deceptive defensive maneuvers. It sets up a real gamelike situation because the blocker may not be able to determine in advance which rusher he must block. Area or zone blocking rules must be established by the coach to instruct offensive linemen as to how they should cope with stunts, blitz, or "games," as these attacks are often referred to. A "blitzing" LBR coupled with a DT or DE can present major problems for offensive linemen.

## CENTER

The link between the offensive line and the offensive backfield is the all-important center. He must be a bright, alert, and tough-minded player. Physically, he falls somewhere between the large tackles and the small guards. His timing, reflexes, and coordination are as vital to offensive success as the deft ball handling of the QB and the elusive running of the HB. He is the clock to the time bomb. If he doesn't get the "ball up" consistently on time, eleven players will not be as effective as they can be.

This reference is to the need for the offensive unit to make the most of its prime advantage over the defense, which is knowing when the ball will be snapped to start the play. It's a well-known fact that when a moving object hits a stationary object (and weights are comparable) the former will best the latter. This principle is the key to the blocker's effectiveness over the defender. If he gets a quick start at the snap of the ball from the center to the QB, he will have a definite edge in the struggle on the LOS. The trigger that fires the blockers is the snap sound from the QB as announced in the huddle. If the QB says the play will start "on 2," then the center must deliver the ball "on 2." If he is a fraction of a second too slow or too late, a quick-starting guard may move forward before the ball moves and an illegal procedure infraction will be called by an official.

If the ball is centered too soon, the offense will be late and the defense, always watching the ball, may get the starting momentum advantage and the play will probably result in failure. The efficiency required of an effective blocking unit can only be obtained when the snap sound from the QB, the forward thrust of the blockers, and the snap of the ball all happen at the same time. It is an action that must be repeated over and over in order to make it happen as routinely as blinking your eyes.

One of the uses a coach derives from a 5- or 7-man blocking sled is to observe the timing performance of his players. As he listens for the snap sound from the QB poised behind the center, he watches the starting movement of the other offensive linemen lined up in front of each blocking dummy on the sled and listens for the sound of the impact of their thrust into the dummies. If he hears one sound, their performance is good. If he hears a few sounds, it may mean a slow launch by some blockers or poor timing of the snap with the snap sound. Many

young centers contribute to this poor timing by not being alert or by not anticipating the snap sound. If the QB says "on 2," the center must be anxiously listening for the sound of the "T" in two and not the "ooo" in two. He must be so eager to hear the sound to snap the ball that he should be coiled like a snake ready to strike.

Choosing a center is just as sensitive as choosing any of the other skill positions. Catching ability of a wide receiver or the throwing ability of a QB is similar in importance to the snapping ability of a center. If the coach is unable to correct and improve on early erratic performance through the use of drills, he should try other players at the position before the season gets under way. Every opportunity to practice the exchange must be seized, such as in passing practice or hand-off practice. A coaching point should be a review of how the center holds the ball, the size of his hand, and the balance of his stance. A large hand may be able to grasp the ball nearer its middle, while a smaller hand may have to move toward the narrower end of the ball. At least two or three fingers should be on the laces, and a wide, stable stance, just like a guard's stance, should enable the ball to come up quickly as the center fires out toward an opponent to perform his blocking assignment. A common mistake is to allow a center to make snaps in practice while he is flat-footed without a forward charge. This does not duplicate game conditions and may cause bad timing to result. An even better technique is to have a defender on the center's nose in full equipment practice sessions to allow the center to fire out at him as he snaps the ball. This is a real simulation of game conditions and will give the coach a good indication of what he can expect when the center performs his vital role for the team.

Snapping for punts, extra points, or field goals requires a wider stance that will permit the center to peer through his legs to determine the direction of his snap. The arms should be fully extended as the body leans gently forward, just barely putting pressure on the ball. The ball should be held with the left hand grasping the top left quarter of the ball while the right cups its fingers under the ball with two or three fingers on the laces. The front nose of the ball should be tilted upward about two or three inches off the ground. This permits the bottom rear of the ball to be firmly pressed on the ground from where it must be lightly scraped through the center's legs as he raises it ever upward on its trajectory into the backfield to the kicker or holder. As the ball comes off the ground, the center must spin the ball with both hands as he spirals it with as much snap and force as he can muster. It is a unique skill that requires a great amount of practice as the center makes minor adjustments on all aspects of his technique until he consistently shoots the ball on its way. Some adjustments to try are: move the legs closer or wider apart, shorten or lengthen the extension of the arms, lower or raise the shoulders from the ground, move one or both hands on the ball, raise the ball sooner or later at the start of the launch, or spin the ball with both hands instead of reliance on the arm with the hand under the ball. Here, too, if a boy doesn't show continued improvement early in his training, keep trying other boys until the best one is found. As a very general rule, taller boys seem to be more capable, probably because of their longer legs and arms which may permit more leverage.

The center's role as a blocker is extremely important because of his proximity to the QB and the origination of every offensive play. Defensive units, particularly below the college level, concentrate a good deal of their special attacks (i.e., stunts, games, etc.) on the areas to either side of the center. A typical maneuver is to bring both middle LBRs up to the LOS and have them blitz through both guard-center gaps in an attempt to tackle the QB as he leaves his starting position after receiving the center's snap. To cope with this kind of unique situation, a center must be quick and bright. He must immediately assess the attack strategy and determine which of the coach's rules he should apply to properly resist the defense.

Although his blocking skills must be equal to the guards and tackles, he has the added responsibility of snapping the ball. To do both effectively, he must keep his head up, neck bowed and eyes alert to the last-second movement of a nose guard or a LBR. As the ball is delivered, he must launch into his block. On punts and place kicks this becomes more difficult because he must sight into the backfield and then steel himself against the onslaught by the defense as they try to block the kick "up the middle." This is the area through which most kicks are blocked. If the center doesn't do his job well, many kicks may be blocked. Here again, the coach may elect to apply a rule that directs each offensive lineman to block the man on his left or right shoulder. Then, he must maintain a balanced position by keeping his legs apart and tail down as he exerts his strength to ward off the defender. He must also be wary of a defensive plan that has the man on his nose pull him forward, forcing him to lose his balance, as a quick LBR rushes through the hole to block the kick. A coach should use this tactic a few times every week as he practices his kick-blocking format against the opposition for that week. Always practice it against your own center to accomplish two purposes, that of blocking kicks and to prepare your center for a similar attack from your opponent.

THE CENTER'S STANCE. With both hands on the ball and weight balanced as he leans slightly forward, the center must snap the ball and quickly block the nose guard out of the play.

# 6

# The Linebacker

In many respects, the LBR is to the defense what the QB is to the offense. He is the key individual, the leader, the spirit and brains of the "tough guys," as many defensive players like to think of themselves. He calls the plays for the defense and is responsible for following the direction and philosophy of the coaching staff. The game plan is reviewed with the LBR to have him understand what the coach wants to do to stop the opponent's offense. As the game proceeds, changes may be made and the LBR must ensure that the defensive unit, which he leads, is attuned to any revised strategy that may be required.

In addition to being an outstanding athlete, a LBR must also be intelligent and strong-minded. His physical traits must include strength, speed, agility, and height. He should be taller than average to help him see over the offensive line as they fire out in their blocking assignments. However, height is not enough. Strength is required to withstand the constant attempts of the offense to drive him out of his location. His area is usually in a gap between his defensive linemen in the varied defensive formations. It is a favorite target for the offense because it does not have one of the big defensive linemen in it. A typical situation is the one in the commonly used 5-2-4 defense.

The LBR may be attacked from the front or from either side. His stance must prepare him to fight off each of these approaches to him as he reads the play and reacts to its strength. The stance most coaches use is the "breakdown" stance where the LBR must put his inside foot about a foot farther back than his outside foot, and must flex his knees to achieve a raised crouch similar to one used by a baseball catcher expecting a base runner to steal on him. His arms should be raised to have his forearms

LINEBACKERS ARE READY. The three linebackers are set for the next offensive play, ready to react to what happens in the backfield.

across the front of his chest with his fists clenched in readiness for battle. At the snap of the ball he should anticipate the forward thrust of an opposing lineman and step up into the hole to defend it. He must try to come up under the charge to straighten up his opponent and take away the strength of his attack. Having done this, he must find the ball and react to the flow of the play.

If he reads "run," he must draw upon his pregame preparation which has informed him of what the opponent likes to do in certain situations. Do they run counter plays, making it look like they're going one way but actually end up going in an opposite direction? Do they use the "draw," faking a pass and then sending a runner slashing up the middle? These and many others may be in the offensive game plan; a good LBR has to know where and when the probabilities may occur.

When the LBR suspects a pass or the down and distance almost predicts one, he should "loosen up," which means cheating back from

his normal one yard off the LOS position to a two- to three-yard depth. This makes it easier to get into his pass defense zone and to read the flow of the receivers, particularly the TE who is nearest to him. In man-to-man pass coverage, the LBR usually covers the running back on his side of the field.

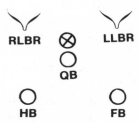

The LLBR would cover the FB and the RLBR the HB in situations where the offense is putting their backs into the pass play. Most of the time short passes are thrown to the backs because the offense's blocking protection is weakened by their release and the QB probably won't have much time to throw the ball anyway. When the back releases immediately, the LBR can usually notice him, but when the back shows pass block and then releases, only an alert LBR will follow him. Another variation of this is when a TE actually pass blocks for a few seconds as he retreats with the other offensive linemen and then releases quickly over the vacated middle for a quick pass from the QB. For these reasons, as a LBR drops back into his "hook zone," the area where receivers run short hook pass patterns, he should seek out and find the whereabouts of the TE and RB to his side to avoid having them surprise him.

Another vital role of the LBR is the pursuit role. Good defensive teams pursue with great enthusiasm. Once you're sure you know where the ball is, chase after it but don't follow a teammate. Take a different angle and attempt to head the runner off on his race toward the goal line. For a LBR, this usually occurs on an end run sweep by the offense. The LBR should direct his reaction to a place on the field where he feels he can get close enough to the ball carrier to tackle him. On a sweep, this might be some distance downfield.

There will be other teammates who will try to tackle the RB in the offensive backfield or at the LOS, but the LBR must realize that his responsibility area on the field will not make it possible to get the RB in those two areas. Every defensive player has his own pursuit angle to take on every play; defensive coaches should practice pursuit reaction often in preseason training. Special emphasis must be put on the reaction of players on the opposite side of the field from the direction of the play. Their pursuit angles often are directed 20 to 30 yards downfield just in case the defenders on the play side of the field miss their tackles. All good defensive teams are good pursuit teams, and the LBR plays a major role.

The LBR is often the leading tackler on the team because he has greater range and freedom than most of his teammates. Whereas the linemen are battering into and through the offensive line, from a three or four point, low stance, the LBR is upright and more elusive as he attempts to ward off blockers and plug up the holes in his line. When the LBR reads the running play to his left or right as in an off-tackle blast, he must come across the LOS and attempt to make the tackle as deep in the offensive backfield as he can.

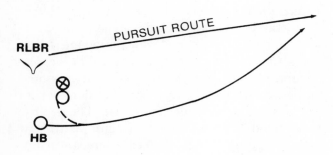

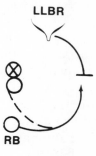

LBR

LBR's

DUMMY   ◯   ◯ DUMMY

◯ DUMMY

◯ BLOCKER

◯ RB

BLOCKERS

RB's

In the same way a RB is taught to look for daylight as he approaches the LOS, the LBR must also look for the same daylight to plug it for the defense. If the LBR gets into the wrong slot, the RB will find no defender when he crosses the LOS. The LBR must not commit himself to a gap unless he's certain it's the daylight the RB is trying to run through. A good drill to practice this requires dummies or pylons to create running lanes.

In this drill, the LBR must parallel the RB's path and, when he turns upfield for yardage, the LBR must turn and meet him in the hole on the LOS. It should be practiced in both directions and may include all defensive backs because they are all faced with similar angle-tackling problems.

Another important LBR tackling drill is the "pit drill."

A running lane is created by the two dummies. A blocker, carrying a lightweight dummy (or without a dummy if one is not available) charges forward toward the LBR as the RB follows him toward the LOS. The LBR steps forward from his breakdown stance, delivers a forearm blow to the dummy, and attempts to cast it aside while he remains in the hole to make the tackle. A variation is to have two or three blockers rushing at the LBR to see if he can keep from being "blown out of the pit" by using a good, low stance and his strength. Players get a big kick out of this drill. To get the most out of it, give each boy a chance "in the pit" and let everyone have a shot with the dummies to knock him over. It's a great morale booster and also shows the coach which players have the strength and toughness he's looking for.

The "quarterback/leadership" role of the LBR not only includes calling the defensive plays but requires him to be an outstanding performer. The LBR has an excellent oportunity to be a key defender because he is usually involved with the stunts and games employed by an imaginative defensive coach. In fact, defensive strategy should include an assortment of such blitzing tactics not only involving LBRs but also other members of the defensive secondary. In each case, they require quickness and timing as well as carefully executed deployment to maintain an element of surprise. The defense must avoid "tipping off" the offense as to how they are going to be attacked. Here are a few typical stunts.

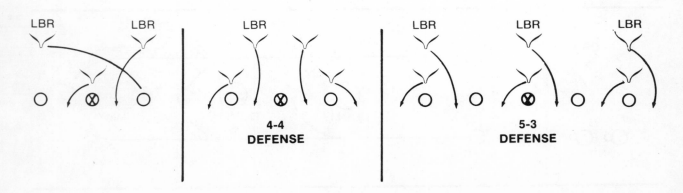

4-4
DEFENSE

5-3
DEFENSE

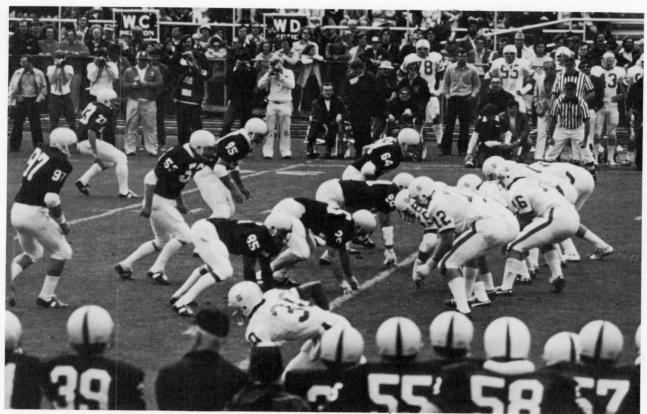

LINEBACKERS' BLITZ. The linebackers start toward the line of scrimmage as the offensive linemen take their first step backward to begin their pass-blocking technique.

THE WARRIOR. Football is a game of hard work in quest of victory.

The LBR must cheat up a little closer to the LOS but not only on stunts. He must keep his eye on the ball and move quickly when he sees the center snap the ball. His arms and hands play an important role because they must fend off the blocks of the offensive linemen as he races into the opponent's backfield. As he penetrates, he must read the flow of the play and react. A successful blitz may result in a significant loss of yardage but there are dangers. Two aspects of good defensive play are weakened by LBR stunts. One is the pursuit strength of the LBR as he roams the field to make open field tackles. If a RB gets through the defensive line, he will only have a few safeties to beat for a long run or a touchdown. The other weakness is the vulnerability to a quick pass to the TE. If the LBR blitzes, a teammate playing opposite the TE must "get a piece of him." This means he must keep the TE from releasing quickly off the LOS. By delaying him with forearm shivers, the

QB will be under pressure from the stunting LBRs and may not have time to throw a completion.

The coaching staff should look for LBR candidates early in the preseason practices by evaluating speed and toughness along with good tackling ability. They are not an abundant breed, and considerable training and development effort will be required. It is also recommended that a LBR be assigned as a team captain to help establish him as a central authority both off the field and on. Football is a game of emotion and example. It can only help a team to be successful if the coaching staff can harness every source of strength and get the most mileage out of it. A LBR captain leader figure can be an immense source of emotion and example for his teammates to follow.

# 7

# The Cornerback/Safety

Many of the qualities of a LBR must be found in the highly skilled positions of cornerback (CB) and safety (S). These players must be tough and they must be good tacklers, but their speed and size requirements are significantly different. The primary role of the C/S positions is to protect against the pass and to react quickly to running plays in time to make tackles on or near the LOS. To do both of these jobs, speed is essential.

When evaluating team personnel, the coach first looks at the running ability and quickness of his players. The fastest runners are usually considered for running-back or defensive-back positions. Among those, the more compactly built should be tried at RB because their heavier muscular structure will permit them to absorb greater physical punishment without serious injury. The slimmer, less muscular boys, particularly the taller ones, should be tried at the demanding C/S positions. Height with speed is

important because they must cover tall, fast receivers such as split ends and tight ends. When there is a height mismatch, a high pass from a QB may be impossible to defend against. However, when a shorter boy with better speed is competing with a slower, tall boy, the speed factor should take precedence.

Although the physical requirements for CB and S are similar, they have slightly different roles to play that may enable the coach to assign his personnel more wisely. The CB frequently must come up to the LOS outside the DE to make the tackle on sweeps. He will also have to contend with the open field blocking of a pulling guard or a lead back which will require him to use his strength to fight off the attack to make the tackle. Therefore, it would be wise to have the stronger, better tacklers play CB because they are subjected to greater rigors at the corners.

It holds then that the more slightly built boys,

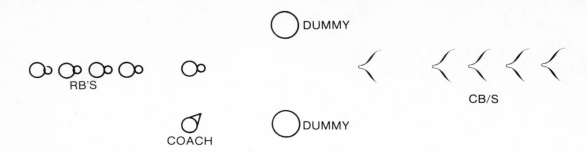

who are usually faster because they are not carrying as much weight, should be safeties and not have to take the continuous punishment near the LOS. Their tackling usually is open field, one-on-one, because most of the interference is used up getting the RB into the secondary. A sure tackle style should be stressed because it may be a touchdown-saving tackle. This should consist of a shoulder-high attack calling for the S to ride the RB down instead of an ankle-high tackle that is frequently missed. It should be assumed that a skilled RB would be a serious threat in an open field and that a high percentage defense should be used. Tackling practice should be a frequent part of CB/S drills to ensure that experience in this vital art is expanded as much as possible. The LBR tackling drill described earlier in this chapter and the one above are good drills.

The boys lie on their backs with their heads facing each other. On the coach's whistle, they both scramble to their feet, turn, and contest one another. The RB must try to run through or around the C/S but must stay within the boundary of the dummies which are about eight feet apart. This one-on-one encounter provides a good game situation for both participants and doesn't risk injury because their starting position minimizes momentum.

Another skill the C/S must possess is the ability to run backward with good speed. This is required to enable him to cover pass receivers without turning his back on them. As covered in the chapter on wide receivers/split ends, a primary objective of a pass route is to make the defender turn. This may allow the WR the split second to alter his pass route while the defender cannot see him. To avoid this, the C/S must go as far and as fast as he can in a backpedal fashion to keep the WR in full view at all times. To do this, frequent practice is required on at least a daily basis. Here again, there are specific drills designed to improve this ability. The first is one that should be part of the entire team's daily running practice. (See below.)

Line the players up two yards apart in rows of five abreast. As they reach the coach, they turn their backs downfield and, at the starting signal, they start running backward. The key coaching point is to make certain they pump their arms in time with their steps because legs will move only as fast as arms stay in unison with them. The players should be urged to take the longest strides possible and to maintain an even pace and rhythm. Frequent practice will yield surprising improvement, even with the bigger, less coordinated boys. It's a great coordination-training technique, and frequent

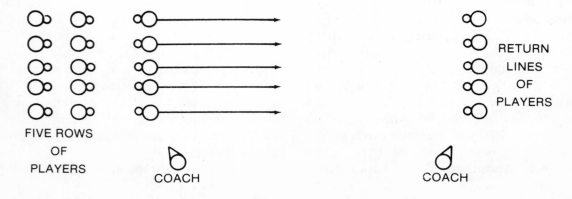

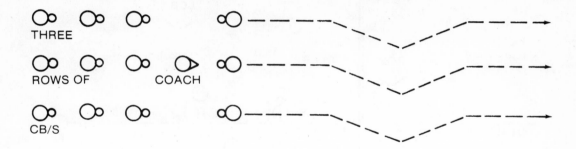

THREE
ROWS OF          COACH
CB/S

falls in early season will almost disappear by midseason. On weekly intervals, races should be held to promote greater effort and interest; the fastest boy should get as much recognition as the fastest conventional runner.

A more difficult drill specifically designed for pass-protection practice is the wave drill (top).

The coach holds a ball over his head and thrusts it at the first group of players, causing them to start backpedaling as fast as they can. To change their path, the coach waves the ball to their left and they change their course to that direction. A coaching point is to show them how to make a crossover step bringing their "away" leg across the other leg toward the direction of the wave. They must continue to run sideways, at an angle, while they keep their eye on the coach. This simulates their need to watch the QB in a game as they maintain their coverage on the WR. Once again the coach waves and they must react to the new direction. A typical series will require the coach to make each group retreat in both directions as well as backward, at the end of which he throws a long, interceptable pass to various parts of the secondary. The boys should call for the catch, avoiding the confusion of two boys interfering with each other, and then return the ball back up the field to return it to the coach. They then return to the end of the line to await their next turn.

Another coaching point is to teach one of the boys to "block back" after the interception. This is used to teach the C/S to anticipate a block on the intended receiver who may be further down-field from the interceptor and is a potential threat to tackle him. It is also effective to instruct the boys to make a special call as they make an interception to alert the entire team that they have the ball. We have used "bandit"

or "bingo" and other two-syllable words that can be bellowed out telling the team to block for the return. It becomes an inspiration that makes the boys try even harder to make an interception.

The proper field position for the C/S often depends on the location of the ball and the score of the game. The CB may line up closer to the DE if the near sideline is at his side but may widen his location if the wide side of the field is on his outside. On the other hand, if his team is a few touchdowns ahead, he may back off the LOS and widen his position in anticipation of a pass. Another consideration is the defensive formation and whether zone or man coverage is required.

In man coverage, for example in a 5-4-2 defense, the CB to the wide side, or "up" side as it is often referred to, has flat-zone responsibility because the secondary rotates to the up side.

RCB          RS                    LS

     RLBR  LLBR        LCB

SE          ⊗  TE
          QB          FL
     HB  FB

The LCB must maintain the required strength to the wide side because it is a logical area for the offense to attack. The man-coverage responsibility is delegated to the RCB (on the SE), the RS (on the TE), and the LS (on the FL). The inside LBRs and the LCB pick up zone-man coverage on the HB and FB or if one of the other receivers runs a short pattern into their area. The four CB/S players would rotate to the other side when it becomes the wide side of the field. When the ball is between the inbound markers in midfield, the defensive captain must precall the up side to allow the C/S group to assume their correct assignments.

A switch in the up call may be required if the offense suddenly sends a man in motion away from the precalled up side. What started as "up left" would have to be called "up right" by the captain when he sees the motion man take off on his route (at top of page).

Having started from the "up left" formation, the entire secondary rotates to "up right," calling for the RS to cover the FL in motion, the LS on the SE, and the LCB on the TE. Once again, the remaining three play man-zone to cover the RBs and the short zones.

Zone coverage results in the same basic rotation of the secondary but assigns them to the zones. In either man or zone coverage the C/S must line up five to seven yards off the LOS on the inside shoulder of the man he's covering. He must quickly determine the speed of the WR and adjust his depth accordingly. A cardinal rule is to never allow a receiver to get behind you, and playing too close to a quick receiver can lead to trouble. A coaching point is to teach the C/S to use the sideline as an ally. When he's playing close to the near sideline, he can afford to play the receiver more "inside-out." This means he can cheat farther in toward the center of the field to take away the probable inside pass route because passes to the short side of the field are infrequent.

As a further technique to help train the C/S to cover receivers, the coach should combine offensive and defensive practice. When the QBs are throwing pass routes to the receivers, the C/S should line up to cover each man as he runs his route.

The QB and WR preplan the pass route in a mini-huddle. After the play is run, all participants return to their original line to wait their next turn. A wider variation of this is to put the entire defensive secondary on the field against the skeleton offensive group. This "skeleton drill" can be practiced with or without full equipment but always with helmets on. It permits full offensive pass plays to be thrown against a full defensive secondary with only a pass rush missing. To compensate for this, the coach should use a stopwatch and blow the whistle when seven seconds have elapsed. Most passes must be thrown in up to seven seconds or the QB will most likely be forced to scramble or will be sacked. Practice of this type involves many players and prepares them for real game-like situations. A fringe benefit for teams that like to throw and practice it frequently is that it also provides their C/S players with a great deal of pass coverage practice; this strengthens the team in an area that most teams are weak in. A defense cannot be strong without excellent players in their defensive perimeter.

# 8

# The Defensive Linemen

## DEFENSIVE END

If a coach begins his search for defensive linemen by picking his biggest and strongest players, the fastest ones should be considered for the all-important position of defensive end (DE). This position requires players with many of the same talents as the LBR. They must be agile and strong, particularly with upper-body strength, because one of their key duties is to fight off blocks by lead backs or pulling linemen. Players must be able to move quickly into the required defensive area and to avoid having their legs and feet contacted by cross-body blocking which would knock them off their feet.

The DE is similar to the tight end in physical requirements. Faced with making a choice, the coach should lean to the boys with "good hands" and better speed for TE; the others should be tried at DE. When these qualities are equal among some candidates, those who are better blockers should be TEs and those who are "tougher" should be assigned to DE.

Toughness in a defensive lineman is required to meet the challenge of the offensive blockers. The DE is often blocked by the equally big OT and TE or the hard-hitting FB who is sometimes asked to ram a shoulder block into the DE to allow the HB to run to daylight. When offenses feature slot and/or tight flanker formations, the DE is placed in a situation where he must anticipate being attacked from three different directions (top of page 48).

Probably the most vulnerable block is the down block because if the offense can seal off the DE, they have a good shot at making a long gain around end. In lower levels of football, end runs are primary weapons of attack. If the coach finds it necessary to position the DE down from a blocker, he must compensate for it

DE

OT            TE

FL

DE

OT            TE

FL

DE

OT            TE

FL

by assigning a CB the responsibility of protecting against an end run. It would be wise to avoid placing the DE in this situation by establishing rules for him to react to. The most common rule is based on the location of the offensive end.

DE

OT ←— 3 YDS —→ TE

CB

DE

O T ←— 4 OR MORE —→ TE
YDS

If the TE splits up to three yards, the DE moves out with him and lines up on his outside eye to be able to resist an attempted down block and to be prepared to fight through an out block as well. However, if the TE splits to four or more yards, the DE should move in and halve the distance between the TE and the OT. In this situation, outside help would be required from a CB.

Another good defensive drill for the DE that can be combined with the offense is the pulling guard drill.

The DE must come across the LOS quickly and low with legs apart for good balance. At a depth of two yards he must set his feet parallel to the LOS with his inside leg forward and his outside leg back in a low crouch. He must then lower his inside shoulder and lean into the blocker's thrust. At the instant of contact, the inside forearm and other hand and arm should come up through the blocker's chest and shoulders to weaken his drive. The DE must then quickly recover in time to meet another block or make the tackle on the RB. This drill simulates a game condition most frequently faced by a DE.

The DE must call on his agility and strength in pass rushing against the offense. Strong arms and shoulders are used to play through a pass blocker by pushing up through his chest and shoulders to make him lose his balance. The DE may place his hands on the blocker's helmet and shoulder pads and shove or pull while alternating his footwork to drive through or around him. However, as he is doing this, he must observe the movements of the QB and adjust the direction of his charge accordingly. In particular, the DE should try to contain the QB toward the center of the defense and not allow him to get outside. Outside defense is vulnerable on a pass play because the CB and the S are downfield guarding pass receivers. If the QB starts to run outside, they may have to come up to tackle the QB and be forced to leave their receiver open for a last-second pass completion. The DE must try to prevent this from happen-

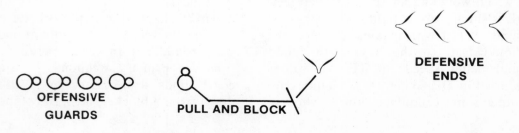

OFFENSIVE
GUARDS

PULL AND BLOCK

DEFENSIVE
ENDS

ing by turning the QB in where other defensive linemen can tackle him. The DE must be a versatile, intelligent athlete to serve his team effectively in many different capacities. He is a key defender.

When playing against a nonsplit set, the DE is usually positioned on the TE's outside shoulder in 5-4, 5-3, and 4-4 type defenses or in a stand-up outside position in some 6-man line defenses. Playing through the outside shoulder of the TE requires a hard, low charge by the DE from a quick release three-point stance. In this role, he is virtually a DT putting pressure on the TE in an attempt to get into the offensive backfield. If he sees the TE trying to release on a pass route, he should try to jam him into the OT or DT to prevent his escape for a quick pass. Outside runs should be forced to the sidelines.

The stand-up DE position, usually seen in a wide-tackle 6-man line, requires a quick two-to-three-yard penetration into the backfield and then a turn to face any oncoming blockers. The rule here is to prevent any end run and force the RB to cut inside the DE where other defenders can make the tackle. By assuring a wide-stanced crouch with his hands low to the ground in front of his legs, the DE can drive blocking attempts at his legs down into the ground to stay on his feet.

## DEFENSIVE TACKLE

The backbone of the defense is the defensive tackle. He is the biggest, strongest, and toughest player on the team. The left DT is the center of the team's left-side defense and the right DT is his counterpart for the right-side defense. They both must cope with the equally big and strong offensive tackles whose main purpose is to neutralize the big men of the defense.

Offensive running plays fall into four major categories. They go inside tackle, outside tackle, trap the tackle, or go around end. Obviously more sophisticated offenses in upper levels (i.e., high school, college, etc.) have a much wider variety and can attack any area on the LOS. But, in lower levels, most of the action gets into the tackle vicinity and the DT is expected to

**DOUBLE TEAM OUT**

**DOUBLE TEAM DOWN**

make many key defensive plays. One of his problems is that he can be double teamed down or out.

In each situation he is met by the low-charging OT whose objective is to get under his chest and drive him up and weaken his thrust. At practically the same instant of contact, either the OG or the TE joins in the block to double the offensive power. It's two against one and, if the DT comes out of his stance high, he'll be driven back on his backside and the play will probably succeed. Because both offensive men attempt to use their shoulder surface to wedge and drive the DT, they must try to attack in unison with equal pressure. To counteract the double team block, the DT must not only stay low but he must also try to split the blockers by attacking one of their shoulders with all the arm and shoulder force he can muster. If successful, he will break the wall and be free to make the tackle. The least he should strive for is to remain in his defensive zone and not be driven out of it.

To meet the rigors of a double team is typical of the role of the DT. The coach must take many steps to assure his team's readiness at this vital position. In his player selection process, the coach must carefully assign his big men properly. He has already taken the big, fast players with pass catching ability and put them at TE. The same type who didn't catch as well became DEs. The very biggest of all, with usually a little less speed but with hopefully more toughness, should be put on the depth chart at DT. All of them must be put through constant agility training because bigness alone is not an excuse to be slow footed. One of the major improvements in football over the last thirty years has been the remarkable improvement in the quickness of the big players. This has been the direct result of the introduction of a wide variety of agility drills (see Chapter 9).

Another important area of improvement has been the development of arm, shoulder, and overall upper-body strength. This has been particularly vital to the DT because his arms are his primary weapons in dealing with the powerful thrusts of the blockers he meets at the LOS. A program of upper-body strengthening must be developed at all levels of play. In professional and college ranks, a wide assortment of weight lifting and strengthening devices are available. Special assignments are given to members of the coaching staff to direct and supervise this activity. Many books are available to control and regulate the duration of each exercise to achieve the required strength levels of each player. Standards are established for various positions, with minor variations based on the height and weight of individual players.

Some of the equipment has now become available in high school football programs, but usually with less provisions. A frequently used device is known as a "Universal Gym," a steel structure with various "stations" or features that permit as few as six or as many as fifteen players to participate in bodybuilding exercises at the same time. If such a facility is not available, normal gym equipment such as horizontal bars, chinning bars, horses, parallel bars, etc., can be used to create a scheduled program of strength-developing exercises. Off-season activity is strongly recommended to provide many

months for the gradual development of body building and the weight gain that accompanies it.

At the lower levels of football, below high school, the coach must be ingenious to develop techniques for increasing the strength of his players. Barbells and weight-lifting equipment must be used carefully. In this area again, special instructional booklets are available to serve as guidelines. Gradual progress is mandatory because of the age and body development of youngsters. Probably the most sensible approach for boys is the use of routine exercises such as pushups, chinning, and many of the hand and arm "isometrics" that are now commonly used at all football levels. The isometric concept merely requires the application of two forces operating against each other. For example, by placing both palms against each other at chest level, pressure applied by both arms to press the palms tightly together pits the muscles of the left arm against those of the right. Maintaining the pressure for ten seconds a few times every day, week after week, will slowly but surely develop arm, shoulder, and chest muscles.

A similar but opposite isometric requires a wrestler's finger grasp of each hand at the same chest-high level and a pulling-apart pressure by both arms. This puts stress on many of the same muscles but also reaches others not affected by the palm press. These are only two of dozens of isometrics that can be obtained from available texts on the subject.

Regardless of the techniques used, upper-body strength is required for all players, particularly defensive personnel and, most importantly, defensive linemen. Once this is included in the recurring practice routine, the coach must work the use of the hands and arms into his DT development program. This can be done by

DEFENSIVE LINEMEN'S STANCE. Left tackle and left end (white jerseys) are ready to charge into right tackle and tight end.

setting up special drills that will help offensive players practice their skills on the strong DTs.

The purpose of the drill is to simulate a game condition for the DT. The coach may position him in the gap between the OG and OT or he may put him "heads-up" on either one. The coach stands behind the DT and points at either the OG or OT to apply a drive or fire block on the DT. The coach also holds up his fingers to indicate the snap sound and then proceeds to initiate the action by calling "set" and then the snap sounds. The DT is required to react to the movement of the OG or OT and then to launch his counterattack.

The DT must start from either a 3- or 4-point stance depending upon either the coach's preference or what the individual player is most effective with. Because he doesn't know which player will attack him, he must be prepared for either or both. His objective is to keep the blockers from reaching his body. To do this, he must meet their initial thrust with an upward stroke of his forearm and hand to the head and/or shoulder of his opponent. As he does this, he must maintain a wide stance by keeping his legs as wide as his shoulders; they must dig and churn to call upon the strength of his huge thigh

muscles to overcome the blocker's strength. The first blow of the forearm must be followed by repeated shivers from both forearms and hands in a continuous attempt to cause the blocker to lose his balance. The hand and arms are the only advantages the DT has because the OT is not permitted to put his hands on the DT's body. If he does, offensive holding is called by an official.

In the above drill, the coach should continue to rotate personnel and take extra care to point out their deficiencies, but he must not forget to praise their accomplishments. A penetration through his blocker is to the DT what a touchdown is to a RB. The coach should not allow too many players to participate in one area. Rather, he should divide them into two groups, on opposite sides of him, to avoid having them standing in line too long. This could result in their cooling off, which increases the risk of injury. While one group is performing, the other group is preparing to perform. They need only wait for the coach to turn around and watch them to trigger their action.

The coach may also vary the blocks deployed against the DT. He may call for pass blocks, crab blocks, and double team blocks. By adding a C and another OG, the coach may also include trap blocking by the off guard. This will make the DT aware that, when his nearest opponents allow him to penetrate without attempting to block him, he must anticipate a block from a remote player such as a trapping guard or back.

Repeated use of this drill will develop the skills of the DT and help make him the key defender he must be to ensure a strong defense against the running game. His agility, strength, and arm techniques will make him effective as a pass rusher to help shut down that offensive weapon, too. The DT is important to the success of the team. A good coach will devote much of his time getting his players ready to fill that role.

## DEFENSIVE GUARD/MIDDLE GUARD

Depending upon the type of defense being used, there is either one defensive guard or two. When there is one, he is referred to as a middle guard (MG); when there are two, they are known as left defensive guard (LDG) and right defensive guard (RDG). The defenses that use a middle guard are known as "odd" defenses because they usually have a 5-man (an odd number) line. Two defensive guards are used in "even" defenses because they are usually 4- or 6-man (even numbered) lines.

The role of the MG differs slightly from that of the DG. He is usually backed by two middle linebackers and the three of them are responsible for shutting off the inside running game of the offense. They are affected slightly by the position of the DTs in the 5-man line, which may result in the LBR's relocation but not the MG.

In the 50 Normal, the MG has inside help from the LLBR and RLBR and may elect to

**50 NORMAL DEFENSE**

**50 EAGLE DEFENSE**

attack the center in a variety of ways. He may make his charge through the C's right shoulder, through his left shoulder, or straight ahead through the C's head. He can be a little reckless, even to the extent of anticipating or guessing where the ball may be going because his backup men will guard his area. In the 50 Eagle, designed to be used when an outside running play or a pass play is expected, the MG is more on his own and has to play a little more conservatively. By moving the LBRs further outside, away from the MG, they are in a better position to get into their hook zones for pass defense and to pursue down the line on sweeps.

To compensate for the movement of the LBRs, the DTs are moved into the OG-OT holes. This adjustment puts them in a better position to protect the area weakened by the movement of the LBRs toward the outside. However, they are both vulnerable to outblocks by the OGs, which would isolate the MG with no backup as the sole guardian of the middle. It would be possible to trap the MG and send a RB quickly into the secondary (page 53, top).

It is for this reason that the MG must be wary in the 50 Eagle or in any other situation when the MLBRs are required to "cheat" away from their normal assignment. The usual tactic by the MG in this situation is to "hit and sit." This technique calls for him to fire into the C's head and shoulders but he should not attempt to penetrate. He should "sit," which means stop and stand right in front of the C, and fight the pressure as the C tries to move him one way or another. Penetration puts a defender in danger

**3-9 TRAP**

**3-0 DRAW**

of being trapped. Sitting removes that risk and also protects against the draw play, which, in a sense, is a trap of all of the defensive linemen because they are encouraged to penetrate as the blockers retreat. Then, as the blockers ride the defenders toward the sideline, the QB hands off to a RB for a jaunt up the middle (above, top).

If the MG races into the offensive backfield, he can be trapped easily by a RB while the QB hands off to the other RB as the DTs and DEs are rushing outside. Sitting protects against it.

Of course, the extra quickness and agility required of the MG can help him recover from many tough situations. The player selection process has already accounted for the DE and DT requirements. They should be tall and strong; the MG may be shorter and strong. It usually follows that shorter players are quicker, and the coach must look for this in his shorter recruits. The MG frequently starts from a four-point stance with both hands on the ground and his legs coiled for an explosive launch into the C. He should keep his eye on the ball, which is right under his nose, and as soon as the C starts the snap, the MG must use his quickness to attack. If he can beat the C off the ball, he may cause the C to lose his balance and get into the backfield in time to hit the QB as he moves away from the C to the hand-off area.

The MG's strength is required to cope with the double team block that he is vulnerable to from either OG. When the offense is trying to attack the middle, they will double team either the MG or the DT, depending upon which player is more difficult to block in their match-ups. A commonly used play is the blast play and it can attack through any uncovered lineman. In this case, it will go through the OG against a 5-2 defense with two blocking variations.

A vital part of the MG's duties is to partici-

## 2-8
## BLAST
## (OR BAM)

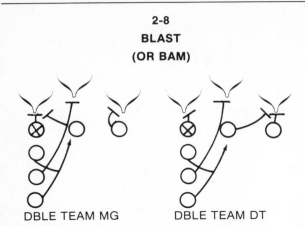

DBLE TEAM MG          DBLE TEAM DT

pate in stunts with the MLBRs. The MG's role is to occupy the offensive man, usually the C, to ensure that while the MG is being blocked, the LBR can enter the offensive backfield. To do his job well, the MG must drive through the C's shoulder on the side opposite to the side the LBR will attack.

As the C blocks to his left, a gap may be created to his right that the LBR may be able to penetrate through to get into the backfield and cause havoc. Although the MG is the decoy in the stunt, he should attempt to penetrate and make the tackle. It's all part of the continuous action to be found at the exciting MG position.

The DG is the same player as the MG. When the team shifts into its "even" defense, if it is a four-man front, the MG usually becomes an inside LBR and the DTs move into the DG posts.

### 4-4 DEFENSE

RCB      RLBR  LLBR    LCB
　DE    DT　　 　DT    　DE

In one of the many variations of the 4-4 above, the coach may elect to move the MG in a 5-2 defense to either of the two MLBR positions or may take him out of the game and replace him. This should only be done when the MG cannot satisfactorily fill the LBR's duties.

Some coaches prefer the six-man front to the 4-4 defense. In this formation, two DGs are used in addition to two DTs and DEs.

### 6-2 DEFENSE

　　　　RLBR　　　　LLBR
DE    DT　 DG      DG 　 DT    DE

The coach may elect to move his regular MLBRs into the DG slots and use his CBs as MLBRs. This would avoid the necessity of sending in substitutes every time a change in defense was desired.

Switching from one defense to another is recommended strongly at all levels but it should not be incorporated in lower levels until the coach is certain the players know one defense well before teaching them another. Having young boys shift from LBR to DG, for instance, may cause confusion regarding the responsibilities of each position. A cardinal principle of defense is to make sure the players clearly understand what their duties are in order to allow them to freely execute without hesitating and wondering about their reaction.

It may often depend on the ability and versatility of the DG as to whether a variety of defenses can be used. He must be a rare talent (in many respects like the MLBR) in order to play different positions—smart enough to confuse the offense with stunts and tough enough to play in the "pit."

# 9

# Agility Drills

As the term implies, agility drills are used to develop quickness, surefootedness, and improved coordination for all team members. An important requirement for agility is overall physical condition. Therefore, in order to achieve the degree of quickness a coach wants in each of his players, he must develop a program of drills designed to bring them to peak condition and, at the same time, improve their coordination. This program must become a regular, daily part of the practice session, encompassing more time in the beginning of the season and gradually decreasing as the season progresses. The drills offered in this chapter are arranged in the order they should be used to achieve the degree of warm-up required for any physical activity. Some changes in sequence can be made as well as substitutions of drills if, in the coach's opinion, they are not suitable for the players involved.

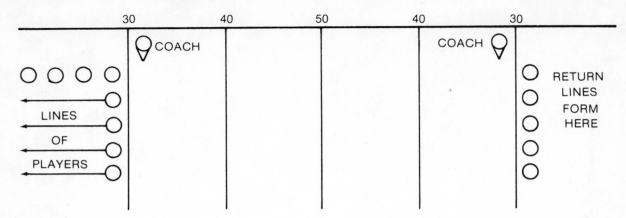

## RUNNING DRILLS

Arrange the players in rows sufficient to give them a few seconds of rest between drills. For example, if there are 30 boys, use five lines with six boys in each. Always try to establish equal numbers, if possible. Have the lines form at the 30-yard line and regroup at the other 30-yard line for their return trip. Be sure to space them apart to avoid having them veer into each other as they move back and forth between the 30-yard lines. All drills begin from each player's starting stance.

## FORM RUNNING

As the players come out of their stance, they assume an upright running position with their chins up, head back, back arched, knees pumping up to waist level in unison with their arms in what is often called "drum major" style. Stride length should be short (one-half yard) because form, not speed, is to be stressed. The purpose of this drill is to teach coordination of leg and arm movements to achieve a smooth rhythm of running. After form running four times back and forth, start the striding drill.

## STRIDING DRILL

This is almost identical to form running except that the length of the stride is exaggeratedly long—as long as the player's legs will allow. In addition, in form running the toes hit the ground first, but in striding, the heels hit first as the fast pace, long strider glides down the field at a bouncing gait. The purpose of this drill is to add bounce and spring to the coordinated leg and arm control in a quickened pace. In this and in any drill, the coach must advise and instruct any boy who may be performing incorrectly. The coach should also look for boys who excel because they may be the candidates for the more highly skilled positions.

## CARIOCA DRILL

Direct the boys to face the sideline, extending their arms toward each goal line with their palms up toward the sky. All five boys should start downfield and try to stay in parallel. As they run sideways, their away leg must alternately be swung in front of and then behind the lead leg.

It will be awkward at first but, with time, even the less coordinated boys will begin to quicken their strides as they run. This drill is probably the best barometer to measure improvement in agility, particularly in the larger, heavier, and/or clumsier players.

## RUNNING BACKWARD

As mentioned in Chapter 6, this drill is also used for defensive safeties and cornerbacks who must become very skilled at backpedaling to keep up with fast receivers. However, it is excellent for improving everyone's agility, especially the big men. The coach would do well to add it to the separate linemen drill routine to accelerate their improvement in this coordination-demanding activity.

## FROG JUMPING

From a slightly crouching position (similar to the pass-blocking crouch), have the boys leap, like a frog, as far as they can. Upon landing, they must not lose their balance and fall forward or backward. Rather, they must quickly recover their balance and leap again as soon and as far as they can. This drill can help improve running speed by building and strengthening the thighs and calves.

## RUN AND TURN DRILL

At the coach's whistle, the players start running at half speed for about 10 yards. A second blast of the whistle signals them to make a 360-degree turn (completely turning around) and continue running for 10 more yards; a third whistle means to turn around again. They then finish the 40-yard course with a full sprint. The coach must direct them to turn to their right going down the field and turn to their left while running up the field. Boys will fall in their early attempts to turn around but will show continued improvement after weeks of practice. The purpose of this drill is to train for full body control in conjunction with balance and running. Progress should be encouraging for less coordinated players as they see their skills improve.

## FULL SPRINT

This is not just a speed running drill. The boys must be told to start from their best balanced stance, to anticipate the starting sound, and to explode forward. The first few steps are very important. They must be taken from the low starting position, but gradually the runner must raise up until he gets to a slight forward lean with his arms pumping away as fast as possible. It will be seen that the players who start more quickly will usually finish first because "catching up" is difficult over a 40-yard distance. Try to keep the boys in line with

others of the same or comparable positions. This will have faster boys (QBs, WRs, RBs) competing with each other while the usually slower positions (Ts, Gs) race against boys their own size. This should be the last of the running drills because it is the most physically demanding. After a week or so of this drill, the team should be ready to be timed officially in their first 40-yard dash against the stopwatch. This should be recorded and repeated a week later and again in midseason when players are usually in their peak form. Records should be kept from year to year to measure the degree of improvement. With young boys whose bodies mature at different ages, sudden improvement may occur at any time.

These drills should be used at the start of practice just after a quick jog around the field. It must be understood that extensive running activity at the beginning of practice may sap all the energy from the players and not allow them to perform well in later activities. At the end of practice, the full sprint may be repeated and alternated with a sprint, jog, sprint drill around four dummies or pylons placed about 20 yards apart in a large square. This should be run for about five minutes before releasing the team for the day. It builds endurance and forces them to run around square corners at full speed; this develops coordination of body lean and running on the edges of the feet. About halfway through this drill the coach should have the boys stop for a few seconds, breathe deeply, and then begin in the opposite direction.

All of the running drills will help increase the speed and stamina of the players. More important, they will become quicker and more agile than they were before they started, and a sound base for good football will be formed.

## CIRCUIT DRILL

A popular innovation designed to make drills more interesting is called the circuit drill. It really is a series of drills put into a rotation plan whereby groups of players move from one activity to another controlled by a coach and a stopwatch. The layout of a plan for this drill should be determined by the availability of

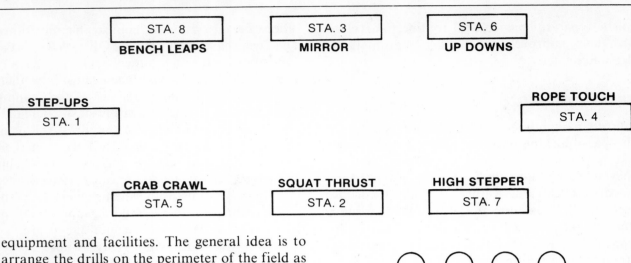

| STA. 8 | STA. 3 | STA. 6 |
| BENCH LEAPS | MIRROR | UP DOWNS |

STEP-UPS

| STA. 1 |

ROPE TOUCH

| STA. 4 |

CRAB CRAWL | SQUAT THRUST | HIGH STEPPER

| STA. 5 | STA. 2 | STA. 7 |

equipment and facilities. The general idea is to arrange the drills on the perimeter of the field as though they were stations on a railroad track that ran around the field. Any area on any field may be used as long as it provides enough space to keep the stations far enough apart from each other to require the players to run from station to station.

Divide the boys into as many groups as you have stations. Assign one boy in each group to act as captain and leader. Direct each group to begin the circuit at a different station. Explain that each group will perform the required activity at each station for a two-minute period, started by the coach's whistle. On the next whistle blast, the captains will lead their "teams" to run to the next station and have them in position to begin the next activity when the coach's whistle signals them to begin. Be certain that all participants clearly understand the requirements at each station. A sample layout could look like the diagram above.

### Station 1—Step-Ups

The boys stand around a bench. They step up with their left leg first and then bring up their right leg to allow them to stand on top of the bench for a second before stepping down. On the next step-up, they start with their other leg first to alternate the stress on each leg. If there is a space problem, as one boy steps down on one side, another boy steps up on the opposite side. Be sure that they stand completely erect when they are on top of the bench to avoid quick dismounts.

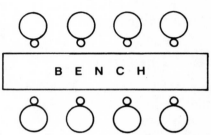

### Station 2—Squat Thrusts

Assuming there are eight boys at each station, arrange them in pairs facing each other. At the starting whistle, each boy drops to a squat position on the ground with his hands and arms down in a pushup position. He then pushes or thrusts his legs back to put him into a full pushup position, pulls them back under his chest, and stands erect. He continues this cycle until the whistle blows to end the session.

### Station 3—Mirror

Arrange the group in pairs facing each other. Establish one side (four of the boys) as the leaders and their opposite partners as their followers. Each of the leaders, at the starting whistle, begins a variety of calisthenics like jumping jacks, toe touches, pushups, quarter turns, etc. As the leader performs, his partner must "mirror" his actions. Other actions like body rolls, stomach rolls, somersaults, hand stands, and just about anything may be used. It's a fun event, and laughs should result from some of the unusual antics. On the next circuit, the leaders and followers switch roles to give the other guys a chance to set an example of quick, difficult movements.

### Station 4—Rope Touch

String a rope at a height a few feet above the reach of the tallest players. It may be attached to a baseball backstop, to the uprights of the goal posts, or to any similar facilities that are available. The boys must be spaced apart so they don't jump on each other. The purpose of this drill is to make the boys leap as high as they can continuously for the two-minute, in station, duration. The drill develops leg muscles and improves coordination and timing.

### Station 5—Crab Crawl

Arrange tires, dummies, or pylons in four pairs; have a boy stand in each space. At the whistle, they drop to an all-four position with only hands and feet on the ground and begin to crawl in between the obstacles, never dropping to their knees. An important coaching point is to have them maintain a fast pace and not allow any boy to become a bottleneck to hold the others back.

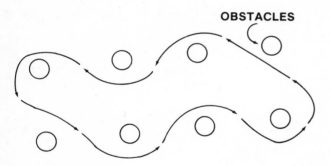

**OBSTACLES**

### Station 6—Up-Downs

Once again the players pair off and face each other a few yards apart. They begin by running in place until the captain drops on his stomach, catching the force of his body on his hands as he hits the ground. Immediately after flattening on the ground, each boy must quickly rise to his feet and continue running in place until the leader drops to the ground again. A key point to stress is to have the boys exaggerate the height of their knees while running in place. They should try to establish an even gait with

knees coming up toward their chins. This is an endurance drill, a leg developer as well as a stomach toughener.

### Station 7—High Stepper

A variety of devices can be obtained to use for the all-important, high-stepping drill. The most common are old tires or dummies laid flat on the ground. A plastic tubes device is on the market but the best is the rope web used by college and professional teams.

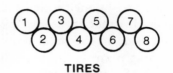

**TIRES**

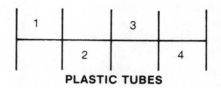

**PLASTIC TUBES**

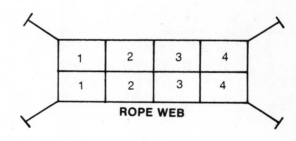

**ROPE WEB**

In any case, the boys must run through these devices with knees high, strict body control, foot control, arms pumping, speed, and balance. If they don't execute well, they will trip and fall. The first time through, their feet hit every hole (see tires above), but in following trips they can race through with four steps (see tubes above) or leapfrog through (see rope web above). There are other patterns like jumping in each hole with both feet or jumping in the second and fourth rows only. It is probably the best single agility, coordination training technique available to teams of all levels and should be used separately for offensive and defensive backs and wide receivers to increase their speed by developing their thigh muscles. The rope web can be made if funds are not available. It requires half-inch rope (or stretch cord), stakes to elevate it about a foot off the ground, and tie-downs to hold it tight in all directions. It's a must for all programs.

### Station 8—Bench Leaps

A bench or board mounted on foot-high boxes or anything similar can be used for this drill. Its purpose is to develop spring in the feet and ankles as well as all the leg muscles. The boys follow each other in a row as the leader leaps from one side to the other over the obstacle. The coaching point is to direct them to stay on their toes while keeping their heels off the ground as they perform. By facing the length of the bench and jumping sideways, they are developing a sense of balance and body control so vital to agility.

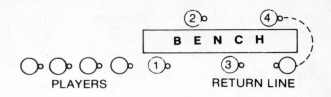

There are dozens of agility drills available for use either in circuit drills or in separate application. The coach must decide which suit his needs based on the requirements of his personnel. If his players are light and quick, he might decide on bodybuilding drills. If they are big and slow, he should incorporate more leg and body control activities into his plan. Allow the time required every day to use some or all of the drills you decide on and make adjustments as you go through the season to reduce the time spent on some and to eliminate others entirely. Only your best judgment can make the most of this important activity in your program.

# 10

# Blocking Techniques

QUARTERBACK PITCH TO RUNNING BACK. The QB
tosses the ball in front of the RB as the offensive linemen
block for the right end sweep.

It is important that an offensive lineman has a clear understanding of each blocking technique and when to apply each. They are his weapons to defeat the enemy; the better he executes them, the more successful he will be. It often takes a coach a long time to realize that winning football must begin with sound blocking and that he must devote a good deal of time, particularly in the beginning of the season, to blocking practice. Observe each player's execution critically and help him improve. Encourage competition among them by grading their performances in early scrimmages and games. Their rewards are not as visible as players at other positions; yet, without their steady, effective services, a successful offense may not be realized. A coach should often praise dedicated effort from all of his players, but he should be particularly free with it to the usually unheralded offensive linemen.

Blocking practice should begin with a review of each boy's stance and his launch style. This may be done with a blocking sled or blocking dummies. Basic style has already been covered in our review of offensive linemen requirements, but the coach must organize his practice schedule to provide time to execute some or all of the following specific blocking techniques. Naturally, the higher the level the more versatile the skills must be.

## FIRE BLOCK

Basic one-on-one block at point of attack. Explode off ball of forward foot; step with back foot. Shoulder initiates contact into numbers—drive, drive, drive! Utilize correct blocking techniques: arched back, short choppy steps, etc. *Block through—not to.*

## REVERSE SHOULDER BLOCK

Utilized when blocking inside gap. Step near foot straight down LOS. Drive outside shoulder into break of leg, head in crotch. Execute proper follow-through techniques. *Block through—not to.*

## NEAR FOOT–NEAR SHOULDER BLOCK

Utilized when blocking man on inside shade or outside shade. Step near foot for crotch, toes pointing straight upfield. Drive near shoulder into break of leg. Execute proper follow-through techniques. *Block through—not to.*

## REACH BLOCK (CRAB)

Utilized when blocking a man to blockers outside in. Can also be applied blocking a man head on or in a shade alignment, but not at point of attack. Drive head and inside elbow past defensive man's outside leg, simultaneously bringing inside leg to crabbing position on outside of defensive man. Scramble, scramble, scramble; strive to get head and body square to goal line. Use pivot and step for takeoff. *Block through—not to.*

## REACH BLOCK (SHOULDER)

Use pivot and step takeoff. Fire head past defensive man's knee, driving inside shoulder into knee. Drive back and regain squared position to goal line. *Block through—not to.*

## POST LEAD BLOCK

Post refers to inside man on double team block. Explode into defensive man, utilizing near foot–near shoulder takeoff. Slip head to inside hip if man head on. Drive man up and straight back. Keep butt to butt with lead blocker. Lead refers to outside man on double teams. Explode shoulder into break of outside leg, utilizing near foot–near shoulder takeoff. Be sure to point step foot for man's crotch with toes straight upfield. Drive man straight back; keep butt to butt with post blocker. It is very important for both blockers to have bodies square to goal line. *Block through—not to.*

## CROSS BLOCK

Executed between on-side guard or tackle. Man going first executes near foot–near shoulder techniques or reverse shoulder techniques. Man going second executes trap pivot and step techniques. *Block through—not to.*

## TRAP

Pivot on away foot step about six inches at a 45-degree angle into hole. Simultaneously pull outside elbow past rib cage and throw away arm past trunk grabbing grass. Drive off step foot and explode up and through defensive man, that is, aim for his inside hip. *Block through—not to.*

## INFLUENCE

Utilized when setting defensive man up for a trap or kick out block by a back. Short jab step with inside foot; pivot and block first man to outside.

## SLAM

A delaying maneuver by pulling linemen to

allow for backfield fake. Short jab step with away foot; count "one thousand one" and go.

## PULL

Pivot on away foot; step lead foot straight down line—90° to LOS. Pull near elbow and throw away arm across body. Drive off step foot; lead ball.

## CRACK BACK

Technique utilized by on-side linemen when blocking first linebacker to inside. Blast at flat angle; do not circle. Drive head in front of linebacker, simultaneously driving your outside shoulder into hip. *Drive through—not to.*

## DOWNFIELD BODY BLOCK

Throw high, not low; strive to put your butt in man's chest. Do not leave feet too quickly. Do not be cautious downfield. Do not look for ball; look for different colored jersey, and blast it.

PRO I DEFENSIVE FORMATION. The split end is to the left, the flanker is to the right, and the halfback is behind the fullback (in white jerseys).

# 11

## Offensive Formations

The question facing every coach is "What offense should I use?" The best decision is the one that matches the talents of the squad. In other words, if there is better running-back talent than passing talent, then a two tight-end offense might be best. If the running backs are the big, strong type without real speed, then a power-oriented formation should be used, such as one of those on page 66, top.

These formations are all strong from end to end, but are not as effective for outside running or for passing as some other formations are. There are some coaches who always use them, however, who would argue the point. It is generally agreed that outside running can best be accomplished from slot or wing sets.

Because of the placement of players toward the outside of the formation, down blocking can be used to spring fast RBs around end behind pulling guards and other backs. Inside running is also available but is not effective because one of the backs is not available for blocking inside because he's located outside.

When we observe the effectiveness of the professional team offenses at throwing the ball, we shouldn't question the strength of spread or split offensive formations for the passing game. The extension of players wide out from the interior linemen forces the defense to spread out to cover them and can result in the isolation of one offensive player on one defensive player. In addition, by spreading the defense, the offense can also attack the middle of the line and achieve some success in doing it. Two of the most popular wide-out formations are illustrated at the bottom of page 66.

A coach can conclude: if you can throw well, use an offense with split ends and flankers but include inside and outside running in your plans. If your throwing is fair and you have

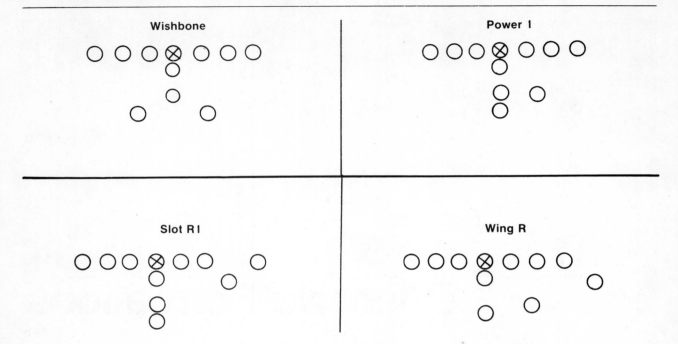

Wishbone    Power I

Slot R I    Wing R

some fast RBs, use a slot or tight flanker set. If throwing is poor, then go for the strongest running formation and concentrate on the basics required for power blocking and running. Notice that the first consideration in each conclusion involved the ability to throw. It has long been accepted that throwing is the quickest way to score so it should be the first area a coach should explore. Next, he should try to exploit any speed talent he may possess and strong power runners.

As a general rule, football for young boys cannot depend on a passing game, because the throwing and catching skills develop gradually. If the boys on your team are up to 11 years old, you should lean toward inside or outside running formations with a few pass plays in your arsenal. Boys from 12 to 14 can be expected to throw the ball with reasonable effectiveness and

can cope with a little more variety in the offense. Above these ages, in junior and senior high school levels and above, players can do it all, and a coach can give them as much as their unique talents can handle.

We're going to focus on inside and outside running plays that can be used at lower levels (8 to 11) and some passing plays that intermediate (12 to 14) levels can use. Our favorite offensive sets are tight and wide slots from which we can run and pass with enough diversification to give even the best defenses a problem.

## INSIDE RUNNING PLAYS

The most effective inside rushing plays are those that hit quickly, have good blocking angles and/or a double team block, and have a lead back blocking ahead of the ball carrier. A

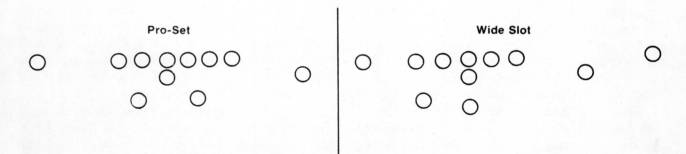

Pro-Set    Wide Slot

THE PRO-SET FORMATION. The defensive secondary must
cover all the way across the field.

A SPREAD OFFENSE. A pass play is about to begin against
a 5-2 Oklahoma defense.

play called the bam or the blast can be directed through many holes on the LOS.

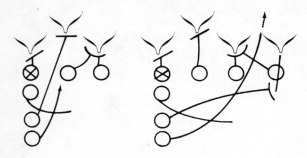

The same kind of play from the wishbone or from the power "I" has the added advantage of having another back in the blocking pattern.

However, that extra back was split out wide in the two-man "I" formation above and required a man to cover him from the defense. When you bring him into the backfield area to block, you also pull the defense closer together.

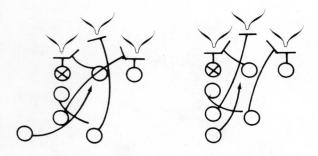

However, if you have the blocking strength on the offensive line and have strong blocking and running backs, you can successfully blow open holes and march down the field.

More simple inside plays are the "quick hitters." They rely on speed and timing as well as sharp, effective blocking in the hole area. They call for the ball carrier to hit the hole quickly without a lead back to block for him. One-on-one blocking in the hole must be executed with fire blocks through the shoulders on the hole side. The back must look for daylight as soon as he hits the hole area.

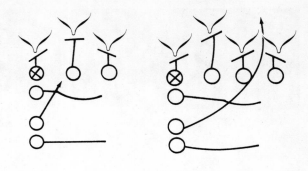

Counter plays are also effective as inside plays, by creating the impression that the ball is going one way while it really is going somewhere else.

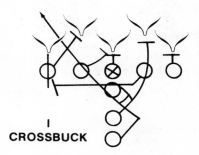

**I**
**CROSSBUCK**

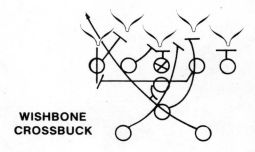

**WISHBONE**
**CROSSBUCK**

Because of the misdirection aspect of the play caused by the fake to another RB, there is enough time available to allow a lineman to pull and trap in the hole area. In lower levels, the defense will usually go after the faking back, and the trap is likely to be successful on the unsuspecting DT. A good counter play is definitely recommended at this and at all other levels too.

## OUTSIDE RUNNING PLAYS

There are a few approaches to outside running. One is the block down and go around everyone. Another is to block down on everyone but the end. Arrange to have him blocked out and run inside of him. The deceptive way is to run a reverse to make it appear the ball is going to the opposite side of the field, only to come back and go outside.

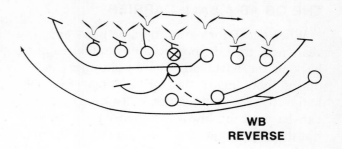

**WB REVERSE**

**HB SWEEP**

The key aspect of the above play is to use the FL to seal off on the DE with a double team on the big DT. The quick pitch to a fast HB and a few blockers out in front will get good yardage. If the defense does not allow you to get outside of them, the "kick-out" block on the end can be successful.

The offensive line must block one on one and encourage the defenders to pursue the apparent sweep. It's important to run some sweeps to make the reverse play look like just another end run. The FL must not start back too soon or he may give the play away. He must allow the HB to get the defense going his way a few steps before taking off for the back hand-off. A pulling guard and the QB can help get the FL around the corner and on his way. The key block is the backside end. If the LE can block him, he should, but if the DE is outside him, the pulling guard or the QB can get him. Another reverse can be run after a fake inside running play. This will attract attention away from the final direction of the play and can use the same overall blocking approach.

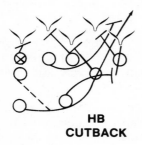

**HB CUTBACK**

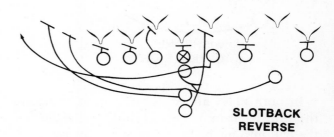

**SLOTBACK REVERSE**

The use of the reverse is generally more successful at the lower levels because less experienced players are more easily fooled, but all the way up to the professional ranks it continues to be a surprise weapon that frequently gains long yardage. There are a wide variety of play designs that can reverse the direction of the ball, but they must all allow the ball to be seen going in the opposite direction before reversing it. This is necessary in order to get the defense to go in the wrong direction.

A good fake by the HB and the QB will make the play successful because they will confuse the defense. The ball carrier on any reverse should be the fastest runner on the team, maybe a WR or a SE. He must be able to use his above average speed to run away from the defenders once they recover from the deception and begin their frantic pursuit.

## THE QB AS A BALL CARRIER

When the T formation became popular many years ago, the QB soon became another running back in the backfield. The development of the option play made the QB a threat to either hand-off, run, or pitch out to a trailing back. It can be used in almost all offensive formations, but the "I" and the wishbone are the most popular.

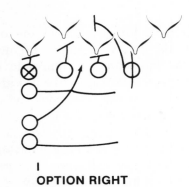

**I
OPTION RIGHT**

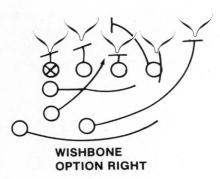

**WISHBONE
OPTION RIGHT**

In both plays above, the QB must ride fake the lead back into the G-T hole. He must put the ball into his belly and go a step or two with it; the QB is covered by the lead back while still maintaining control of the ball. As he leaves the first back, the QB must "read" the DE. This means he must interpret the attack plan of the DE.

If he comes at the QB to tackle him, the QB must quickly pitch a lateral to the HB. If the DE goes toward the HB, the QB should turn upfield and run to daylight. The DE is not blocked because he becomes the "option" man and is put in a squeeze. The option play requires

QUARTERBACK OPTION TECHNIQUE. With both hands on the ball to protect it, the QB looks to pitch to the trailing halfback if the defense tries to tackle him.

a great deal of practice to allow all participants to perform automatically and with deception and speed.

The QB can also be used on bootleg plays. These are based on the same concepts used on the reverse plays. It must appear that the ball is going elsewhere to allow the QB to fake, keep the ball, and run to some other area.

In both plays a good fake is required to misdirect the defense while a pulling guard gets out in front of the ball carrier. The fake must be prolonged by the RB long after the QB leaves him to encourage the defense to follow him and not the QB. Probably the most successful lower-level bootleg play is known as the naked bootleg where the QB goes the opposite way all by himself.

The QB must keep the ball hidden behind his body (on his side) and depend on the element of

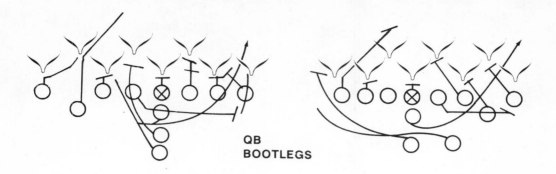

**QB BOOTLEGS**

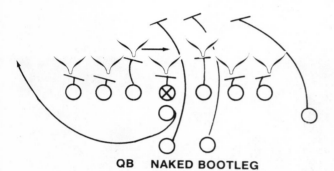

**QB NAKED BOOTLEG**

surprise and his quickness to get around the DE. The coach should look for a DE who gets careless and doesn't come across the LOS when the ball appears to be going away from him. Young DEs often "fall asleep" and can be taken advantage of by a quick, good-faking QB.

QUARTERBACK BOOTLEG PLAY. With the running backs going to the left, the QB races around right end with the ball on his hip to hide it from the defense.

HUDDLE. The team gathers together to listen to the QB call
the next offensive play.

# 12

# A Coach's Playbook

In order to gain a decided advantage over your opponents and force them to a great deal of preparation to set up their defenses to stop you, the use of multiple offenses is strongly recommended. In this playbook you will use a multiple I and strong set offense. You will line up in a two-man I formation and then either stay in it or shift out of it into one of the other formations.

The huddle is the launch area that starts the offense on its way. It must be a well-disciplined part of a team's performance. The players must be able to hear the QB's call of the play, and they must be able to exit to their offensive positions when the huddle breaks up. An efficient huddle can easily be arranged, as the diagram above illustrates.

The QB calls the play and the snap sound. The C, TE, SE, and FL immediately leave and run to their positions. The QB repeats the call and snap sound and he and the remaining players clap their hands, holler "break," and rush to their positions. It must be pointed out that a team that conducts its huddle with poise and precision usually is a team with pride in itself, one that wants to look good as well as be good. Therefore, when the players enter the huddle, they must take care to form it evenly, put their hands on their knees, and keep their backs and heads erect. When the QB calls "break," it's a signal to explode out of the huddle with spirit and enthusiasm—and a chance to show the other team that they're up against a first-class team that knows how to do everything well.

When the HB and FB leave the huddle, they should line up in a stack behind the QB. The FB will be two yards behind the QB and the HB one yard behind the FB, both in an upright stance with their hands on their knees. All the other players will be at their proper positions in two-point stances in the formation the QB called in the huddle. The QB, after seeing that everyone is at their position, calls "get down." The HB and FB will quickly scramble to their set positions. If the QB had called an I set, they stay where they are with the FB dropping into a three-point stance, while the HB remains upright in his two-point stance. This enables him to see over the FB to observe the QB and the entire offense and defense. If the call was a strong right or strong left set, they both assume three-point stances. The linemen drop into their three-point stances on the "get down" call.

The QB must delay long enough for the HB and FB to get to their set positions and for the others to get set before he calls "roll it," which is the final signal before beginning the snap sounds. He then begins the snap sounds, using the word "go" for each sound. In other words, if he said "on the second sound" in the huddle, he would say "go . . . go" and the C would snap the ball as soon as he heard the second "go."

There is some disagreement about how to time the snap sounds called by the QB. Some coaches prefer rhythmic sounds, but most use nonrhythmic because it has proved to be more effective in getting the team "off the ball" together. This means to get the team to start together with no one leaving too soon to cause an "illegal procedure" penalty. If the calls are rhythmic, each player has his own timing as to when the next sound will be, and some players

sometimes may be ahead of the QB's timing. When using nonrhythmic calls, the players have to be ready to move when they hear the next sound and *only* when they hear it. Therefore, they shouldn't launch sooner than required unless they forgot the snap sound.

When the team huddle is formed, the QB will call three sets of numbers. The first set will be the formation number 1 or 22, etc. The second number will be the ball carrier's number, 2 for the HB, 3 for the FB, etc. The third number will be the hole number which is the place between the offensive linemen where the ball carrier will attempt to run with the ball. For example, 8 is between the RG and RT. Therefore, an example of a play would be 128, which means the 1 formation with the HB running through the 8 hole. The linemen must learn their blocking assignments at or near the hole, utilizing one of the various blocking techniques covered in Chapter 10.

Some plays have a name associated with them such as bam, sweep, quick, etc. These will help the players remember their blocking and ball-handling assignments. Pass plays are called with either specific play numbers such as 1181, 22F35 (F means fake), etc. However, other passes may be called by the QB with the pass route numbers (1 through 9).

The following multiple-offense sets and complete set of running and passing plays can serve as the basis for your offense. They may be used at all three levels: 8–11, 12–14, and 15 and up. These cover pre–high school and high school.

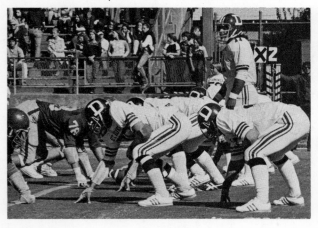

22 STRONG RIGHT OFFENSE. A sweep around right end awaits the QB's snap sound as he looks over his offense.

QUARTERBACK REVIEWS THE DEFENSE. The QB looks over the defense and audibles a new play call to exploit a defensive weakness.

# PLAYBOOK OFFENSIVE FORMATIONS

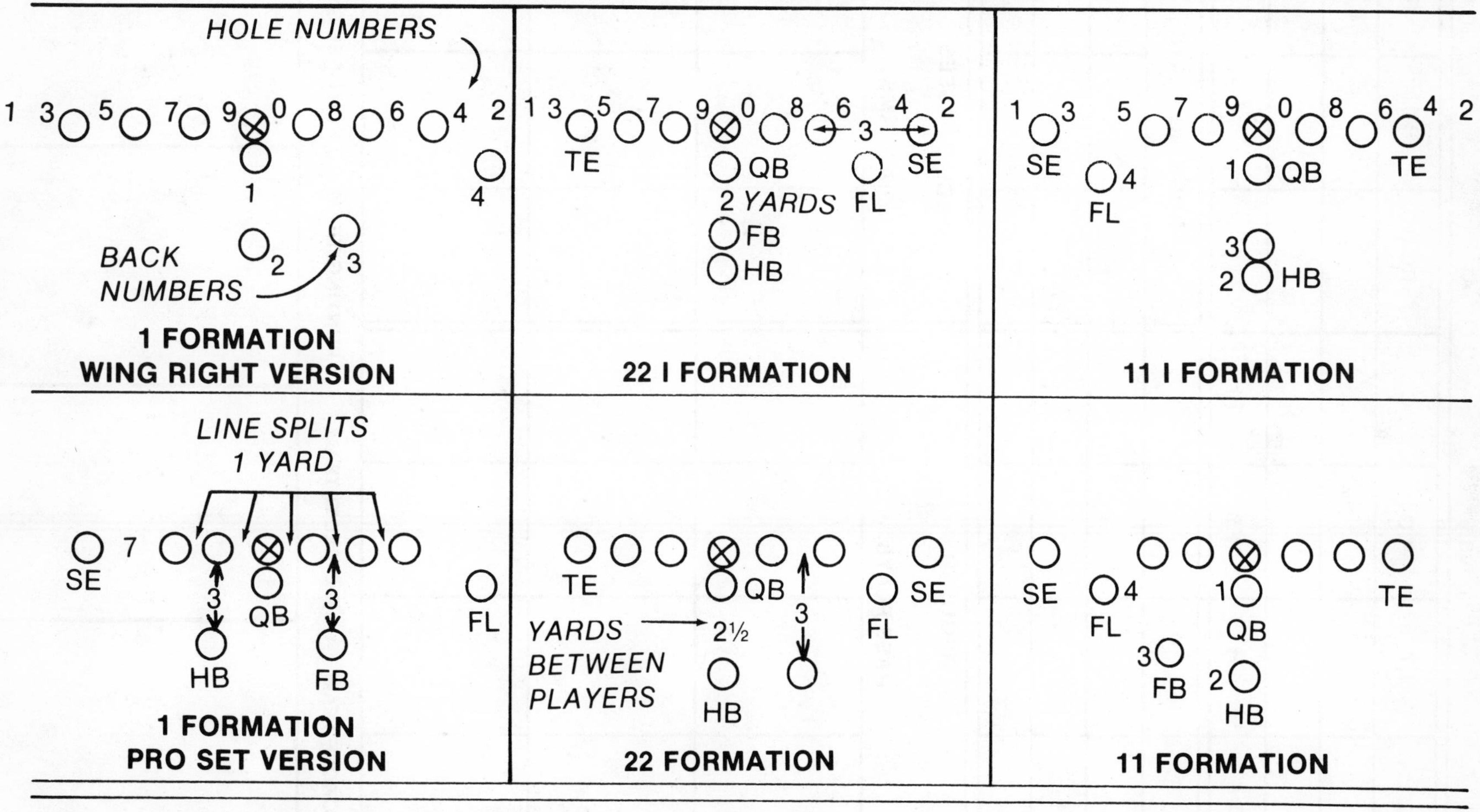

HOLE NUMBERS

BACK NUMBERS

**1 FORMATION**
**WING RIGHT VERSION**

LINE SPLITS
1 YARD

SE   HB   QB   FB   FL

**1 FORMATION**
**PRO SET VERSION**

TE   QB   FB   HB   SE   FL
2 YARDS

**22 I FORMATION**

TE   QB   HB   SE   FL
2½
YARDS → BETWEEN PLAYERS

**22 FORMATION**

SE   FL   QB   HB   TE

**11 I FORMATION**

SE   FL   QB   FB   HB   TE

**11 FORMATION**

| VS | | | | AT | | DATE |
|---|---|---|---|---|---|---|
| LE | LT | LG | C | RG | RT | RE |
| | | | | | | |
| | | | | | | |
| QB | LH | FB | RH | | | |

| | | | | RUNNING PLAYS | | |
|---|---|---|---|---|---|---|
| | | | | | | |
| | | | | | | |
| | | | | | | |

| REGULAR<br><br>PASS PLAYS | | | SPECIAL PASSES<br><br>DIAGRAMS | | |
|---|---|---|---|---|---|
| | | | | | |
| | | | | | |
| | | | | | |

| KICKOFF TEAM | K-O REC'G TEAM | PUNTING TEAM | PUNT REC'G TEAM |
|---|---|---|---|
| | | | |

**OFFENSIVE GAME-PLAN SHEET**

## WING RIGHT VERSION
## 1 FORMATION RUNNING PLAYS VS. AN ODD DEFENSE
### WING RIGHT FORMATION BLOCKING MAY BE USED FOR PRO SET

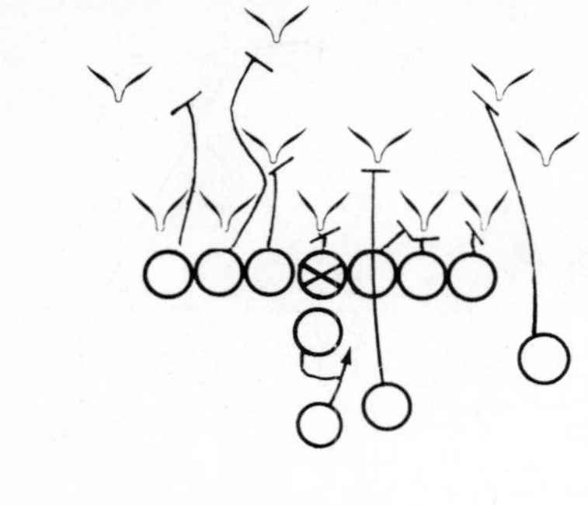

**128 BAM**

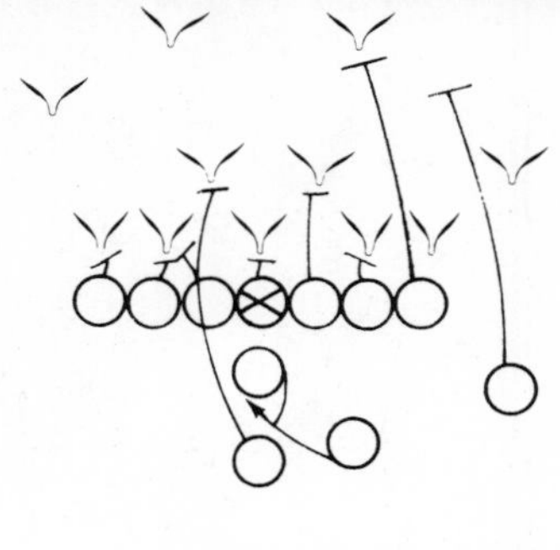

**137 BAM**

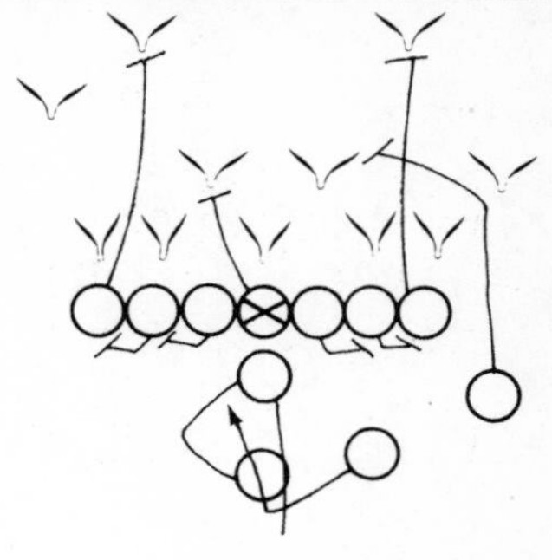

**130 DRAW**

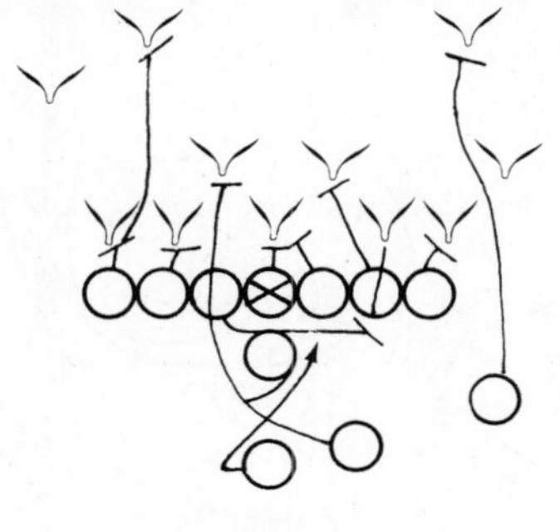

**128 X-BUCK**

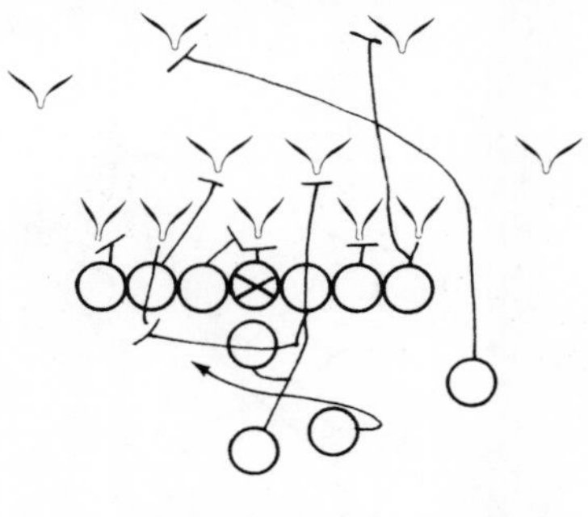

**137 X-BUCK**

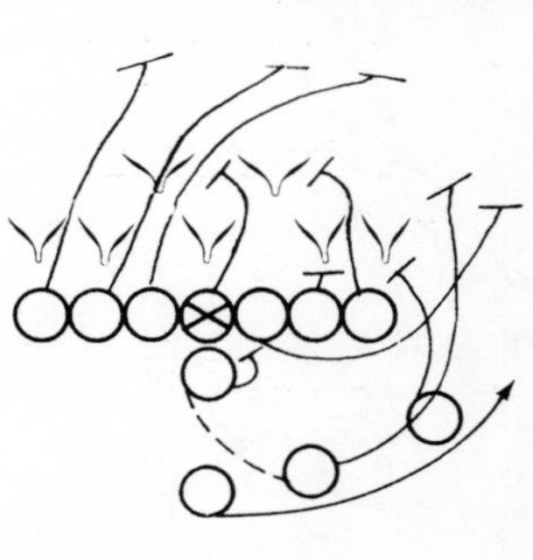

**122 SWEEP**

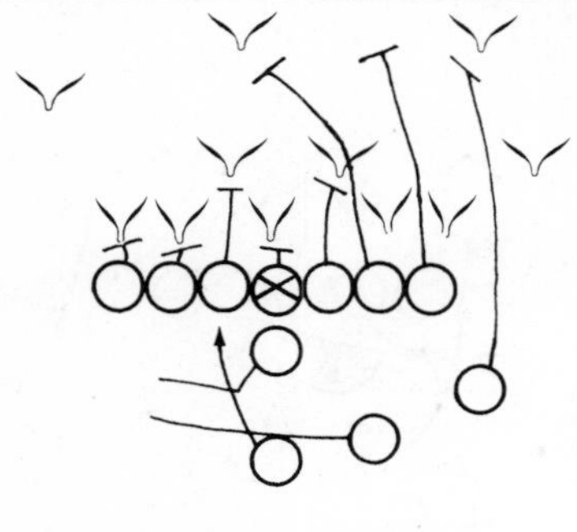

**127 QUICK**

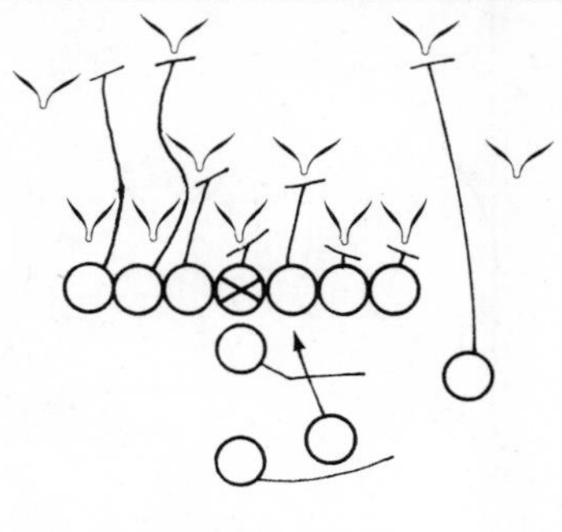

**138 QUICK**

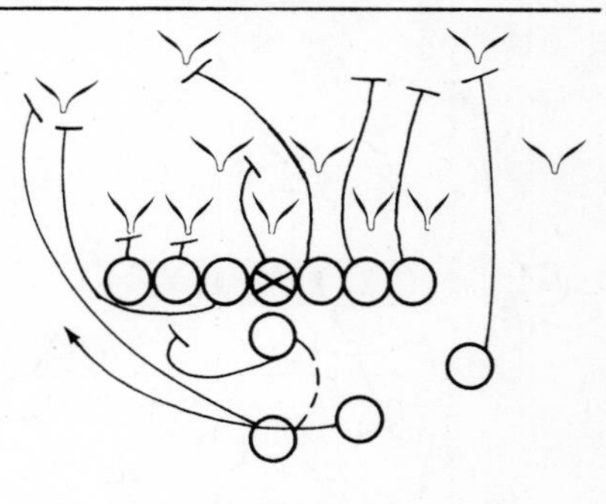

**131 SWEEP**

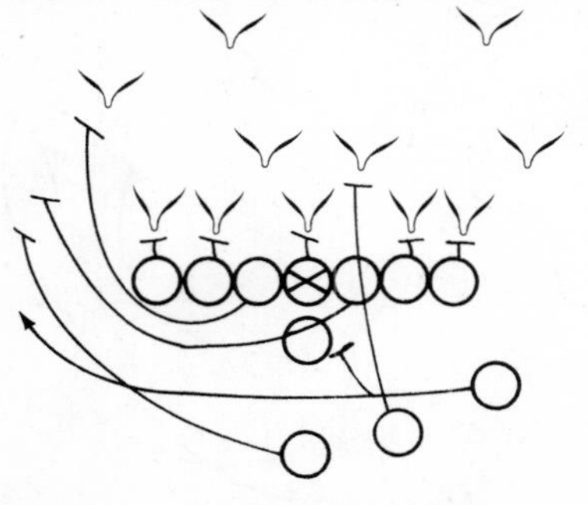

**141 REVERSE**

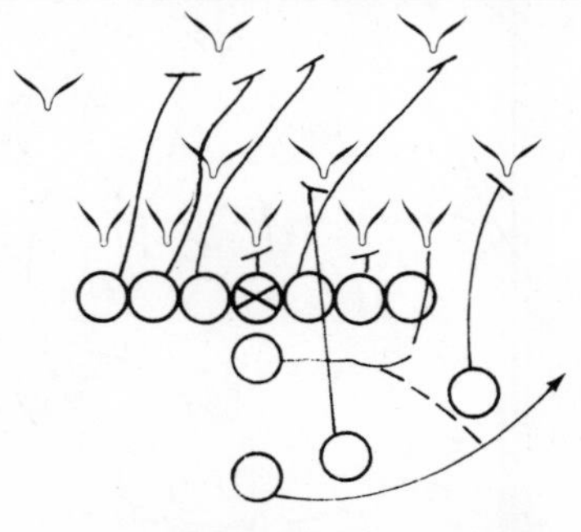

**112 OPTION**

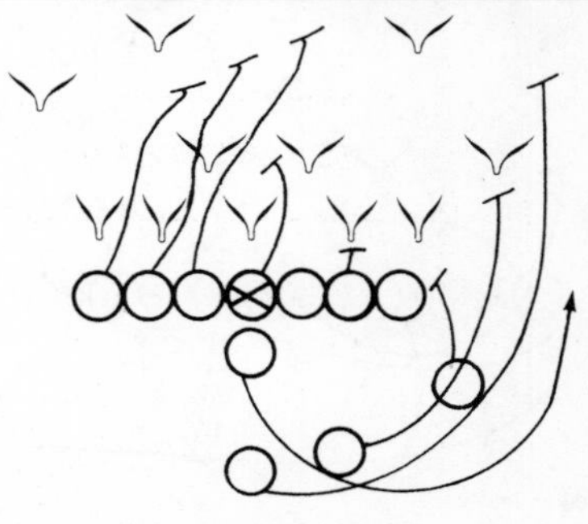

**112 SWEEP**

## THE WING RIGHT VERSION OF THE 1 FORMATION IS MORE
## SUITABLE FOR USE IN LOWER LEVELS. BLOCKING IS THE SAME.

# PRO SET VERSION
## 1 FORMATION RUNNING PLAYS VS. AN EVEN DEFENSE
### PRO SET FORMATION BLOCKING MAY BE USED FOR WING RIGHT

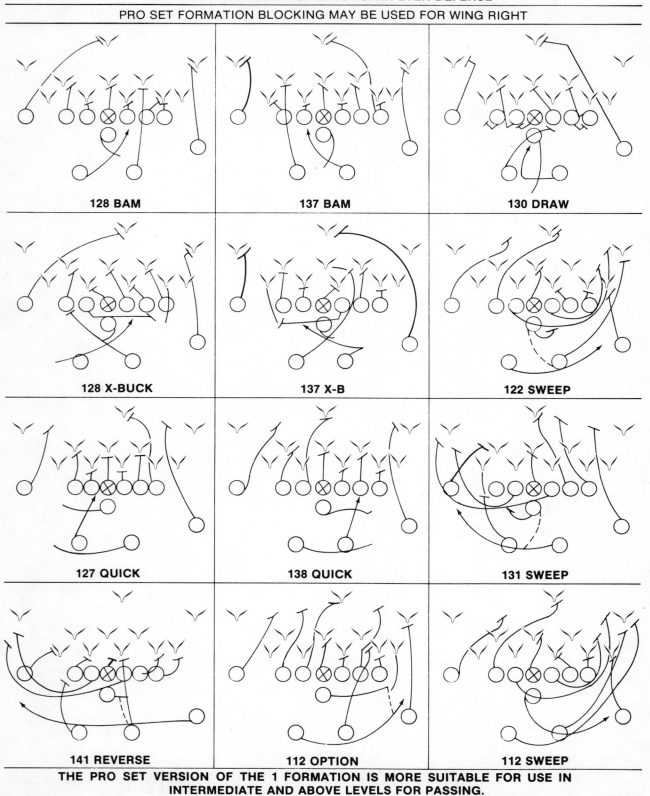

| 128 BAM | 137 BAM | 130 DRAW |
| 128 X-BUCK | 137 X-B | 122 SWEEP |
| 127 QUICK | 138 QUICK | 131 SWEEP |
| 141 REVERSE | 112 OPTION | 112 SWEEP |

## THE PRO SET VERSION OF THE 1 FORMATION IS MORE SUITABLE FOR USE IN INTERMEDIATE AND ABOVE LEVELS FOR PASSING.

## 11 AND 22 FORMATION RUNNING PLAYS VS. AN ODD DEFENSE

### 11 I AND 22 I FORMATIONS MAY USE THE SAME BLOCKING

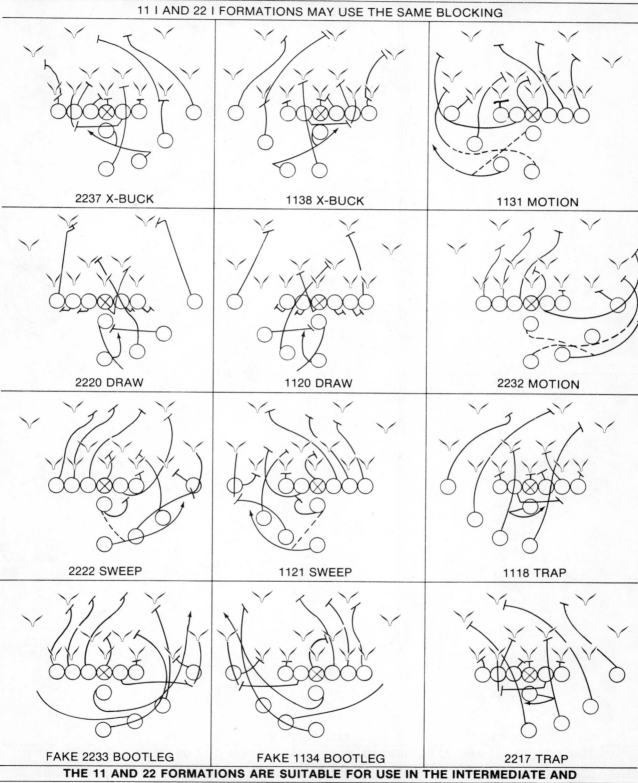

| 2237 X-BUCK | 1138 X-BUCK | 1131 MOTION |
| 2220 DRAW | 1120 DRAW | 2232 MOTION |
| 2222 SWEEP | 1121 SWEEP | 1118 TRAP |
| FAKE 2233 BOOTLEG | FAKE 1134 BOOTLEG | 2217 TRAP |

## THE 11 AND 22 FORMATIONS ARE SUITABLE FOR USE IN THE INTERMEDIATE AND ABOVE LEVELS, AND GOOD LOWER LEVEL TEAMS.

## 11 AND 22 FORMATION RUNNING PLAYS VS. AN EVEN DEFENSE

### 11I AND 22I FORMATIONS MAY USE THE SAME BLOCKING

2237 X-BUCK

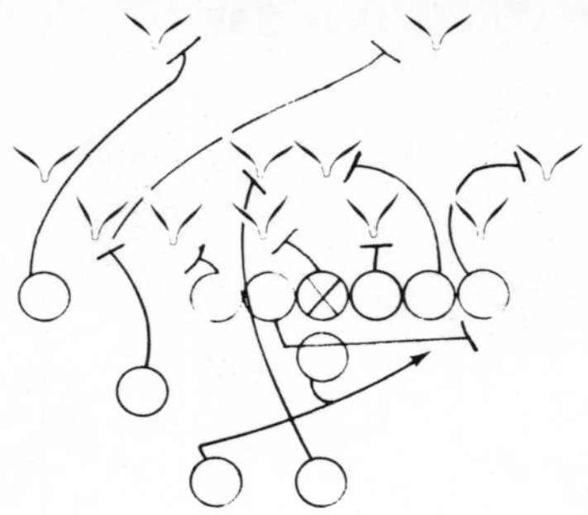

1138 X-BUCK

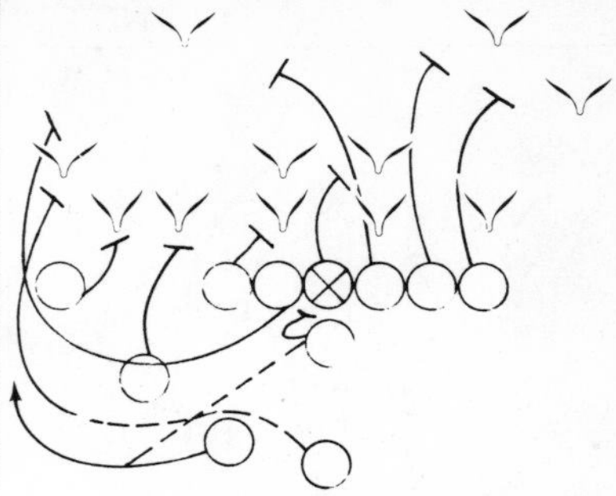

1131 MOTION
ON 2ND SOUND

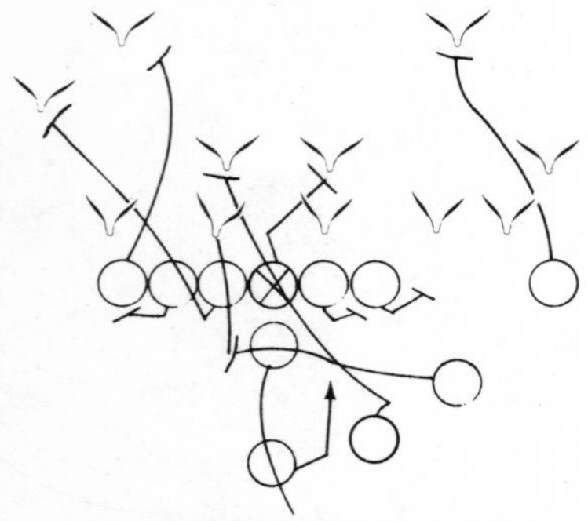

2220 DRAW

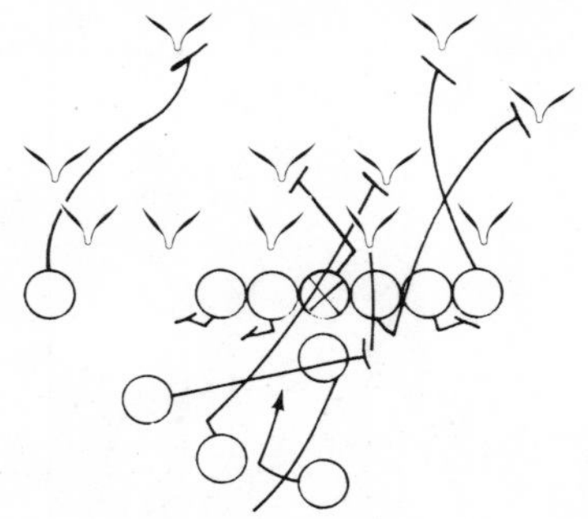

1120 DRAW

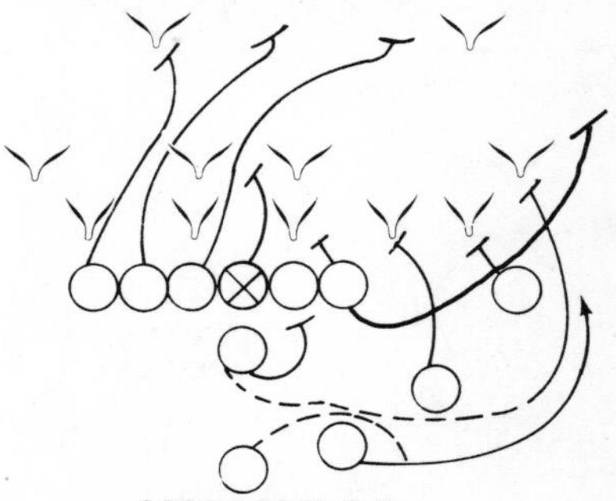

2232 MOTION
ON 2ND SOUND

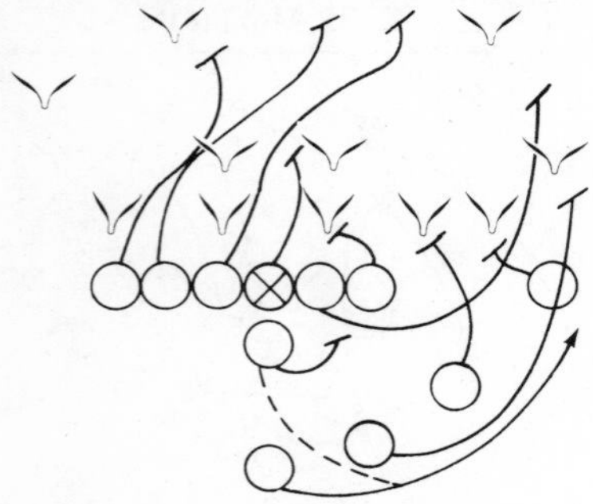

2222 SWEEP

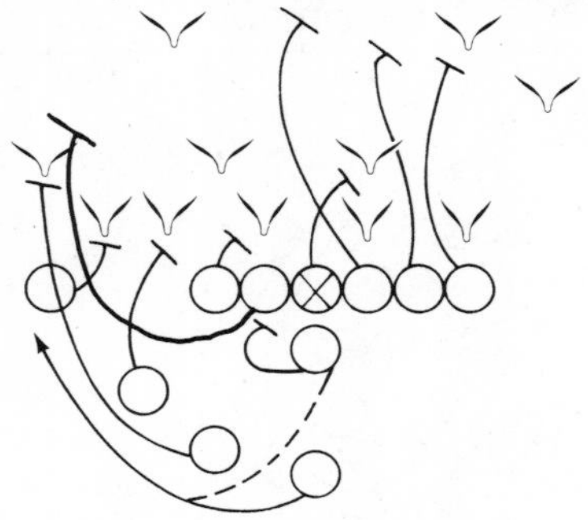

1121 SWEEP

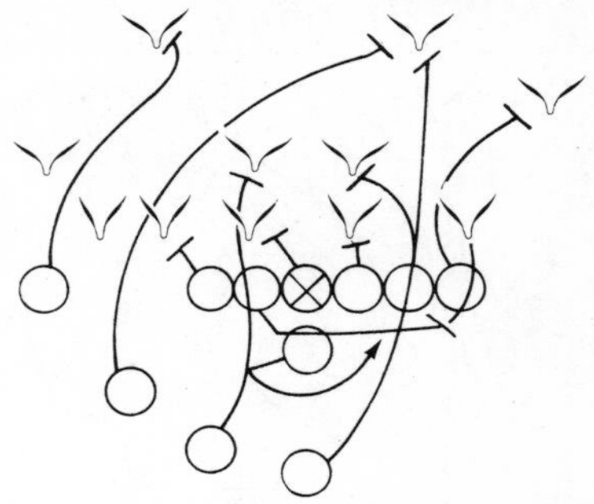

1118 TRAP

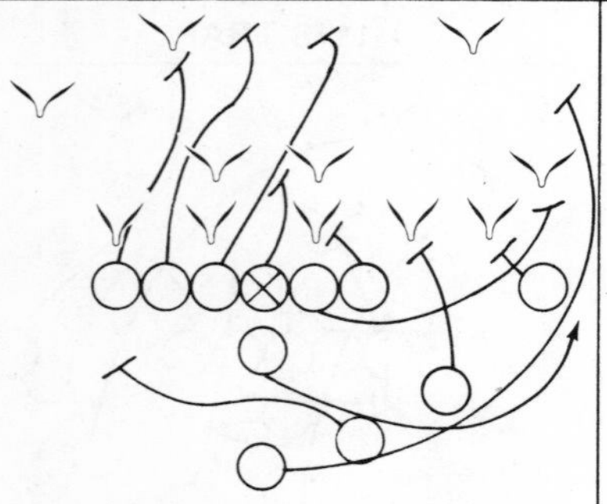

FAKE 2233 BOOTLEG

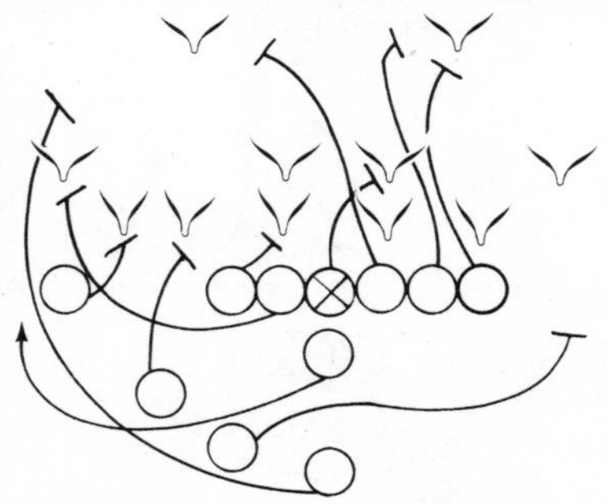

FAKE 1134 BOOTLEG

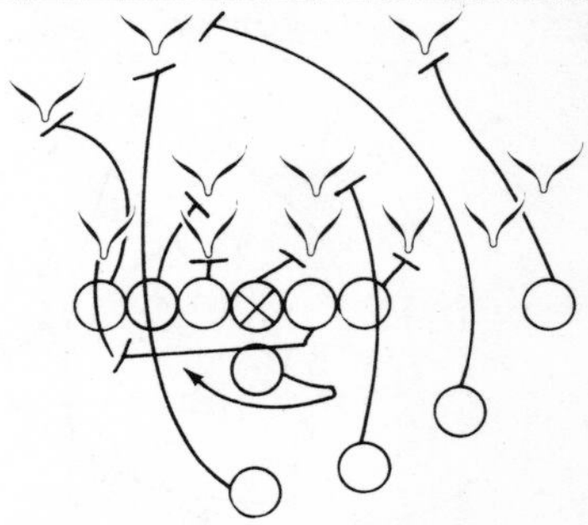

2217 TRAP

## MANY OF THE 11 AND 22 FORMATION PLAYS MAY BE RUN OUT OF THE 11I AND 22I FORMATIONS WITH OR WITHOUT ADJUSTMENTS.

## 11I AND 22I FORMATION RUNNING PLAYS VS. AN ODD DEFENSE
## 11 AND 22 FORMATIONS MAY USE THE SAME BLOCKING

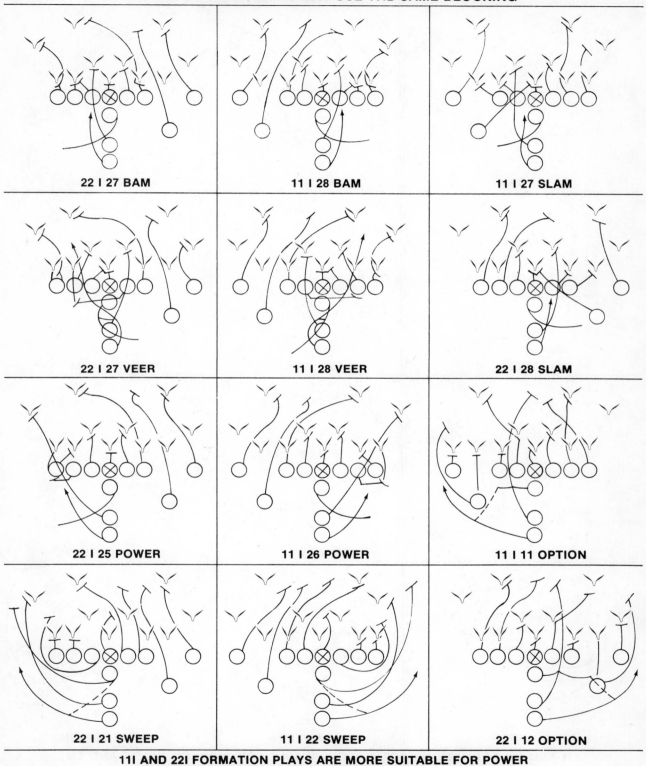

| 22 I 27 BAM | 11 I 28 BAM | 11 I 27 SLAM |

| 22 I 27 VEER | 11 I 28 VEER | 22 I 28 SLAM |

| 22 I 25 POWER | 11 I 26 POWER | 11 I 11 OPTION |

| 22 I 21 SWEEP | 11 I 22 SWEEP | 22 I 12 OPTION |

## 11I AND 22I FORMATION PLAYS ARE MORE SUITABLE FOR POWER
## RUNNING BACKS AND GOOD TRAPPING LINEMEN ON THE LOS

## 11I AND 22I FORMATION RUNNING PLAYS VS. AN EVEN DEFENSE
### 11 AND 22 FORMATIONS MAY USE THE SAME BLOCKING

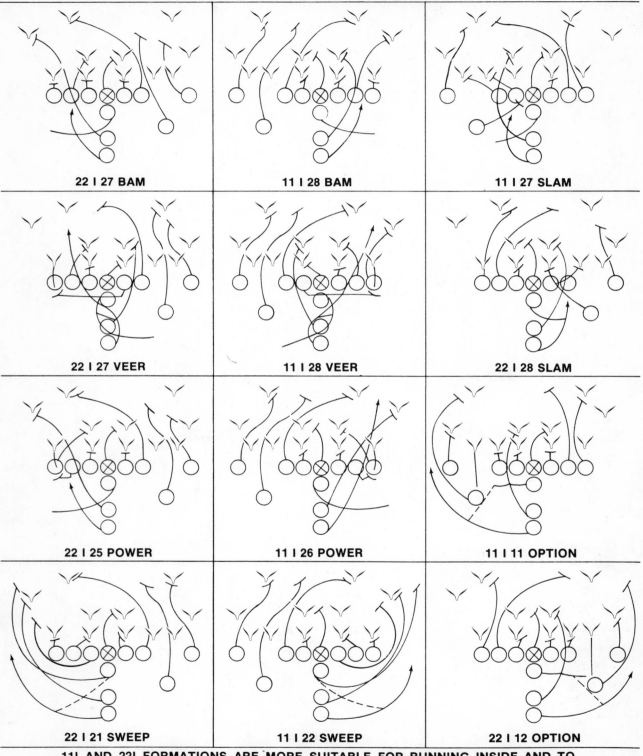

| | | |
|---|---|---|
| **22 I 27 BAM** | **11 I 28 BAM** | **11 I 27 SLAM** |
| **22 I 27 VEER** | **11 I 28 VEER** | **22 I 28 SLAM** |
| **22 I 25 POWER** | **11 I 26 POWER** | **11 I 11 OPTION** |
| **22 I 21 SWEEP** | **11 I 22 SWEEP** | **22 I 12 OPTION** |

## 11I AND 22I FORMATIONS ARE MORE SUITABLE FOR RUNNING INSIDE AND TO THE WEAK SIDE THAN THE 11 AND 22 FORMATIONS

# 11 AND 22 FORMATION PASS PLAYS BY RECEIVER PRIORITY
## 1181, 2, 3, 4 AND 2281, 2, 3, 4 MAY BE THROWN FROM 11I AND 22I FORMATIONS

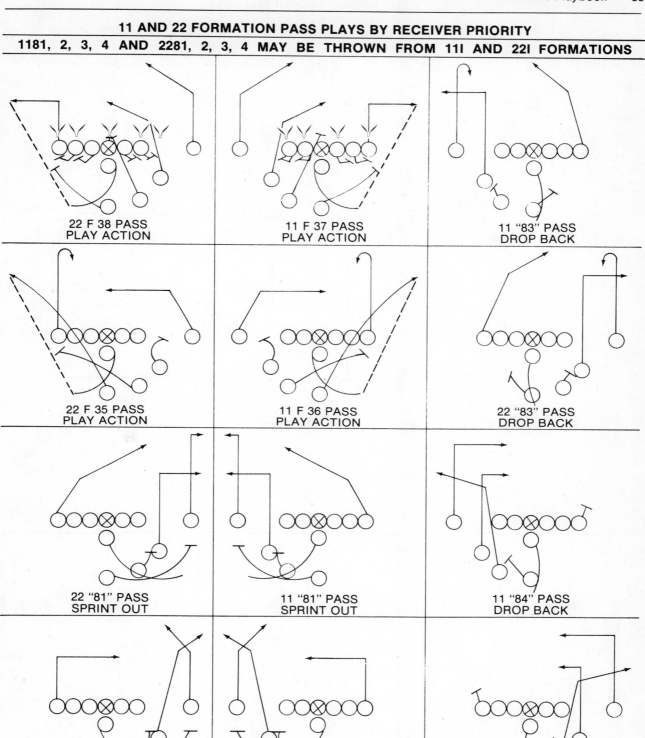

22 F 38 PASS
PLAY ACTION

11 F 37 PASS
PLAY ACTION

11 "83" PASS
DROP BACK

22 F 35 PASS
PLAY ACTION

11 F 36 PASS
PLAY ACTION

22 "83" PASS
DROP BACK

22 "81" PASS
SPRINT OUT

11 "81" PASS
SPRINT OUT

11 "84" PASS
DROP BACK

22 "82" PASS
SPRINT OUT

11 "82" PASS
SPRINT OUT

22 "84" PASS
DROP BACK

## IF OPPONENT'S PASS RUSH IS TOO STRONG TO CONTAIN, ALL
## 80 SERIES PASSES MAY BE THROWN OUT OF SPRINT OUTS

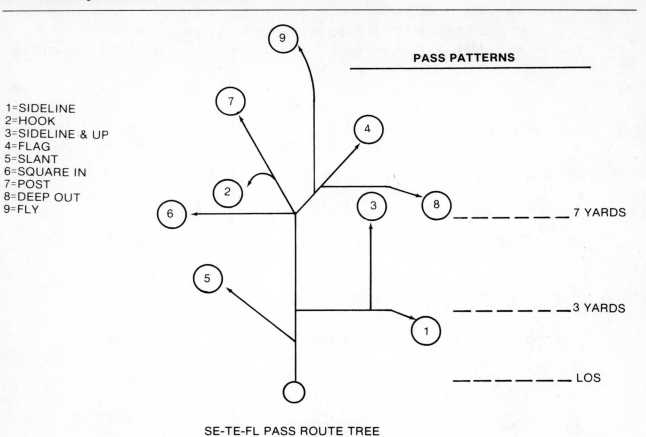

**PASS PATTERNS**

1=SIDELINE
2=HOOK
3=SIDELINE & UP
4=FLAG
5=SLANT
6=SQUARE IN
7=POST
8=DEEP OUT
9=FLY

— — — — — — — 7 YARDS

— — — — — — — 3 YARDS

— — — — — — — LOS

SE-TE-FL PASS ROUTE TREE

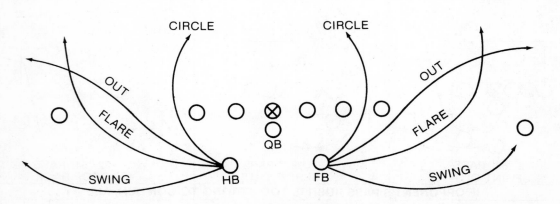

**BACK PASS PATTERNS**

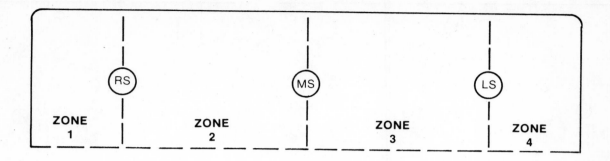

## COMBINATION PASS PATTERNS

A combination, or "combo," pass pattern is one that requires two receivers in order to complete a pass. This means that one receiver serves as a decoy in order to clear a zone which will allow the second receiver to catch a pass in a vacated zone.

"Combo" patterns require a quick study of the opponent's defensive secondary. Most teams play a 3-deep pass zone defense. This creates 4 pass zone areas for us to throw into (above).

Zones 1 to 4 above are the most desirable places to throw a pass. In order to get into those areas, it sometimes will be necessary to slightly adjust our pass routes. For example, in order for the tight end to get into zone 2 on a 7 pattern, he would have to run diagonally toward the middle safety and then slant into zone 2.

The distance downfield that a pass receiver must run will also vary on "combo" patterns. Therefore, it is necessary to determine how to beat the defense by running a short or long pass route. This is also important when you are trying to throw to a back into a zone that has been cleared by one of the three receivers.

In all cases, a "combo" pattern requires a lead receiver and a trailing receiver. If the lead man does not do his job correctly, the trailer will not get open. Receivers must study the attached pass patterns carefully and take the time necessary to learn the pass routes they will have to run as either a lead receiver or a trailer.

Most of the time you should be throwing to the trailer "underneath" the leader. For example, on no. 1 on the pass route sheet, a 789 is designed to hit the TE on an 8 pattern after the FL has taken the LS "up" the field to allow the TE to catch the pass "under" the LS's zone 4. If you are a lead receiver, you must run right at the defender to make sure he sees you. You must also make sure you stay in his zone; if you don't he'll let you go. The trailer must also get to the passing zone as soon as he can, *after* the lead man has cleared it. This requires timing on each play! There is a special problem with the flat and hook zones because they are not too deep. For example, on the 513 the FL must take the cornerback all the way to the sideline before turning upfield. If he turns up too soon, the CB will stay in the middle of his zone and the TE will be covered. The same happens on the 105. The SE must take the CB to the sideline to let the backs get open.

In the above-referenced play numbers (789, etc.) each number represents the pass routes that the three receivers will run. The numbers read left to right; the first route (7) will be run by the first receiver to our left. The next route (8) will be run by the middle receiver, and the last pattern (9) run by the receiver to our right. In this fashion, the coach and QB can create any pass play simply by calling three numbers to match the desired patterns. The following are a variety of combo pass patterns:

## COMBINATION "COMBO" PASS PATTERNS—PRO SET

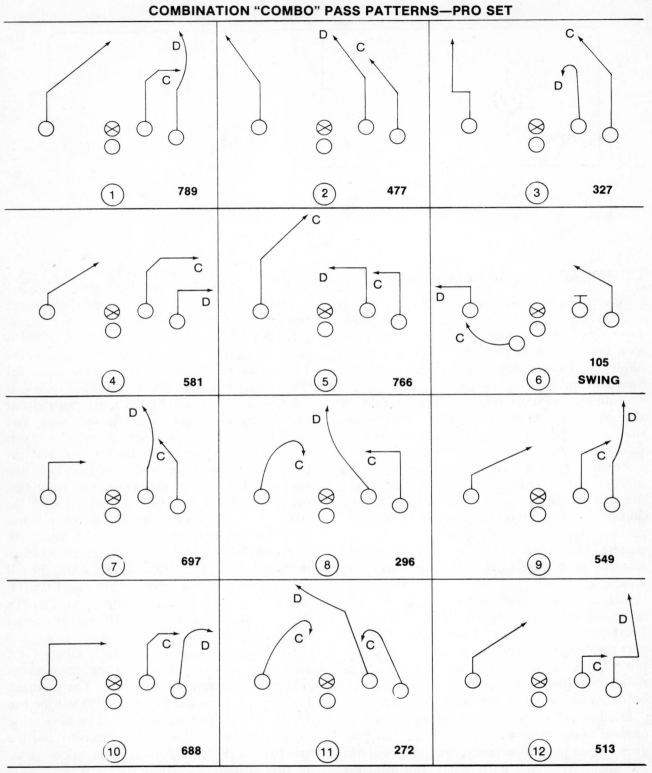

**D=DECOY     C=COMBO MAN**

# 13

# Defensive Techniques

## LINE AND LBR TECHNIQUES

There are many specific techniques that the coach must prepare his defensive players to use. We have identified the physical qualities required for each position and have covered the strength and agility requirements. Now it is necessary to explain and show the defensive player how to use his talents to bring about the desired result—stopping the offense.

### Reading the Head

This is the ability of the defensive man to read the offensive blocker in determining what area the play is attacking. In most instances the offensive man will lead with his head when blocking or try to keep his head between the ball carrier and the defensive man. The defensive man must have the ability to read the offensive blocker, fight the pressure, and get to the point of attack.

### Defeating the Double Team

In defeating the double team we are going to split it or stay low enough to hold the ground we're on and not get driven down the line. The most important thing in defeating the double team is to play the post blocker first. Never play both blockers at the same time. When splitting the double team, a defensive man will play into the post blocker first. As you feel the pressure from the outside, try to drop your outside shoulder and get under the lead blocker. Keep your feet moving; using your arms and hands, try to split the blockers apart, wedging your body between them. If the lead blocker gets his shoulder under yours, bring your elbow down hard into his side, again trying to split the blockers and trying to drive them apart. You must not be driven down the line and off the ground that you occupy. If you feel yourself being taken by the double team, drop to all fours and try to hold your ground. As you do this, continue fighting the pressure, and work to gain more ground.

## Playing the Trap

As the trap or J block is read, we want the defensive man to shuffle to the inside to meet the blocker. Always attempt to keep the inside leg up and the outside leg back. Drop the inside shoulder and deliver a blow with the inside arm, bringing the off hand to the blocker's head or shoulders. Try to close the hole with the offensive blocker; always remember to keep the outside leg back and the shoulders square with the line in order to be able to react back to the outside if the hole is closed and the ball carrier breaks back to the outside.

## Pass Rush

There are several very important elements in pass rush. Quickness is most important. You must get off on the first movement of the offensive man and get to him before he sets up. The next important thing is the use of the hands. You must get your hands on him and not get too close, so as to get tied up with the blocker. Try to turn the blocker; with your feet moving, make your move by the blocker squaring up and continuing your rush. When the passer raises the ball, raise your hands; don't leave your feet. Run through him, putting your chest against his. The four moves we use to get by the offensive blocker are:

### Drive

Put your hands high on the pads of the offensive blocker. Drive him back and into the passer.

### Arm Drag

After getting your hands on the offensive blocker, push with one arm on his shoulder pad and pull the opposite elbow with the off hand. Step to his side, pulling him by you. Square up and continue to rush.

### Swim

After you have engaged the blocker with your hands, strike a blow to his head, pushing it to the side. Reach across with your off hand, pulling yourself by him, squaring up and continuing your rush.

### Hit and Go

The approach to the protector is very important in using this technique. The rusher should work to one side of the protector and concentrate his attention on that shoulder. This should make the protector slide to protect this area, thus getting the offensive man slightly off balance and opening an area to the right or left. If the rusher wants to go to the right, he should drive to his left and then thrust the right hand (open) hard to the shoulder pad of the protector. With the offensive man off balance, the rusher utilizes the same escape technique of driving his left arm over the protector's head while pushing off with the elbow of his arm as he slips by the blocker.

## DEFENSIVE SECONDARY TECHNIQUES

### Up Cornerback

The up corner is the one who is lined up three yards outside of our defensive end and one yard in back of the line of scrimmage.

### Key:

The offensive end on your side of the field, and then the direction of the ball.

1. If the end blocks and the ball comes toward you, move up fast and play for a run.

2. If the end releases and the ball comes toward you, drop off and cover the flat.

3. If the end releases and the ball goes backward, cover the flat.

4. If the ball moves away from you, cover the deep zone away from the action of the ball.

## Back Cornerback

The back corner should be lined up three yards outside of our defensive end, and three yards behind the line of scrimmage. Corners always key end and ball direction.

*Key:*

The offensive end on your side of the field, and then the direction of the ball.

1. If the end blocks and the ball comes toward you, come up fast and play for a run.
2. If the end releases and the ball comes toward you, play the flat for a possible pass play.
3. If the end releases and the ball goes backward for a drop-back pass, cover the deep outside.
4. If the ball goes away from you, cover the deep backside zone.

## Safeties

The safeties line up eight to ten yards deep behind the offensive tackles depending on down and distance and your relative speed to go back.

*Keys:*

The offensive end and wing in front of your side of the field; after you have diagnosed the moves of the keys, locate the direction of the ball.

1. If the end and the wing release (or either) and the ball goes backward:
   a. The safety adjacent to the up corner covers the deep outside third of the field.
   b. The safety adjacent to the back corner covers the deep middle zone.
2. If the end and the wing block, and there is lateral action of the ball:
   a. The safety toward the action of the ball should move up and play for the run.
   b. The safety away from the action of the ball should sprint and cover the deep outside half of the field to the side of the action.
3. If the end or the wing releases and there is lateral action of the ball:
   a. The safety to the action side of the ball covers the deep outside third of the field.
   b. The safety away from the action of the ball covers the deep middle of the field.

Remember: you must find the direction of the ball before you can fulfill your obligation to the defense. If for some reason you cannot find the ball, go back.

# 14

# Defensive Formation

There are many different defensive formations that are used at all levels of football, each designed to cope with the general aspects of the game. Some are better against the running game; others contend more favorably with a passing attack. Depending at which level you are coaching, the formations you use should be those that provide you with the best advantages against your usual opponents.

At the lower age groups, we have already established that the passing game is not likely to be a major offensive weapon. That automatically adjusts our defensive thinking away from a pass-oriented formation to a run-preventing defense. Our next thought should evaluate the strength of the running attacks we meet. Does our opposition run outside effectively? Do they rip long gains between the ends? Do they do one in certain situations and the other only when

they need short yardage? Your conclusions must lead you to a decision that may include two or more defensive formations. If it does, you must be careful to make it easy for the team to switch from one to the other without too much confusion. Particularly where young boys are involved, keep it simple. They should spend most of their time learning how to execute and only a little time learning where to be and special things to do.

Football leagues for the youngest boys probably run outside more than inside because speed and only a little blocking is required. Running inside usually requires a minimum of three blocks to get the RB long yardage gains. Therefore, most coaches at this level stress protecting against end runs. The best defenses for this are the six-man line defenses. Because passes are not usually a threat, there's no need to keep three men deep, so why not have three LBRs and only two safeties? The tight tackle (TT) 6-3-2, therefore, is the best recommendation against a balanced offense.

**TIGHT TACKLE
6-3-2**

If the offense shifts personnel to one side of their formation, the defense must also make adjustments.

**WIDE TACKLE
6-3-2 (LBR's OVER)**

The wide tackle (WT) 6-3-2 above is better suited to cope with a wing back because it takes away the down block he would have on the DE in the TT6. It also allows the LBRs to shift to the strength side of the offense to get them in better position to make a defensive play on runs around end or toward the WB.

If the offense begins to get the advantage on the defense, the coach must again make adjustments. He may elect to have his LBRs stunt with his linemen, or he may have his line "loop" or slant through the offensive line. This is, in effect, a lineman stunt.

In the slant left above, the LBRs must protect the areas left weakened by the looping linemen. In special situations, the LBR's stunts may be combined with the above slant; only the LBRs must attempt to penetrate the gaps left open by their linemen. When stunts and loops fail to stop the opponent's offense, a change in defensive formation is dictated, one that has a completely different look. The game of matching offense to defense is like a military encounter between armies. If one force doesn't know what to expect from another force and doesn't know how to cope with it, an advantage will be had. If you can come up with a defense that the offense doesn't expect, you can confuse them and disrupt their game plan.

A natural change from an even defense such as the 6-2-3 or 6-3-2 is an odd defense. This

**5-4-2
SLANT TOWARD POWER**

**5-3-3
BALANCED ATTACK**

FIVE-MAN ODD DEFENSIVE FORMATION. Two middle linebackers and secondary covering wide receivers.

places defenders in positions somewhat different than the even defenses and provides different stunt possibilities to confuse the offense. This is particularly true of a 5-4-2 or 5-3-3 because stacked LBRs can play havoc with an offense.

However, when you're coaching in an intermediate age limit (12 to 14) and there is more passing to contend with, some of the defensive strength must be shifted from the LOS to the secondary. Care must be taken not to weaken the LOS any more than necessary and yet, attention must be given to wide receivers and the passing game. We believe there's a defense that can do this and do it well. It's the 5-2-4 and we're going to review it in much detail. It can be used at all levels, but is especially recommended at the 12 to 14 and the 15 and older levels. We call it the "50 Normal."

BACK CORNER

FREE SAFETY

STRONG SAFETY

UP CORNER

RLBR     LLBR

RE  RT     MG     LT  LE

**50 NORMAL**

## RESPONSIBILITIES BY POSITION

### Middle Guard

*Alignment:*

Head on C, six to twelve inches off the ball. Three-point stance. Destroy C's block with forearm and/or hand shiver and locate the ball. Read C's head and follow flow of the ball.

*Rules:*

1. If the play is toward the C, hang tough and do not get blown out.
2. If the play is away, pursue; do not run around the C.
3. If the QB drops back, delay and play draw.

### Tackles

*Alignment:*

Outside eye of offensive tackle. If the OT takes a wide split, move to the G-T gap. Three-point stance. Explode into OT with inside forearm keeping him off your LBR. Read OT's block and key movement of the ball.

*Rules:*

1. If the play is toward OT, play OT's charge, locate the ball, and pursue.

2. If the play is away, pursue; do not run around the blocker.
3. If the QB drops back, rush passer from inside.

### Ends

*Alignment:*

Outside shoulder of TE. Split difference if the E is split wider than six yards; come back and play normal. Three-point stance.

*Rules:*

1. If the TE blocks down, look for sweep.
2. If the TE blocks out, look for off-tackle.
3. Force everything outside; never let the ball carrier turn upfield.
4. If the ball goes away, look for reverse and screen.

### Linebackers

*Alignment:*

Head up the OG with feet about two yards off the LOS. Assume breakdown stance and key the OG.

*Rules:*

1. If the OG comes, meet him in the hole with

**50 NORMAL**

PASS RUSH   UP RIGHT

PASS RUSH   UP LEFT

the forearm and/or hand shiver to destroy his block.

2. If the OG pulls, follow him down the LOS as he will lead you to the ball.
3. If the flow is away from you, check for a counter and then pursue. Do not overrun the RB. Get some depth in your pursuit.
4. If the OG shows pass block, go to hook zone. Check flat because of responsibility for a screen pass (opposite, below).

## Up Corner

*Alignment:*

Three yards outside DE and one yard off the LOS.

*Rules:*

1. If the E blocks and the ball comes, move up fast and play for a run.

DEFENSIVE PURSUIT. The defensive team converges on the ball carrier from all directions to stop his forward advance.

2. If the E releases and the ball comes, drop off and cover the flat.
3. If the E releases and the QB drops back, cover the flat.
4. If the ball moves away, drop off and cover the deep outside third away from the action of the play.

## Back Corner

*Alignment:*

Three yards outside DE and three yards off the LOS.

*Rules:*

1. Key the E and ball direction.
2. If the E blocks and the ball comes, come up fast and plan for a run.
3. If the E releases and the ball comes toward you, play the flat for a pass.

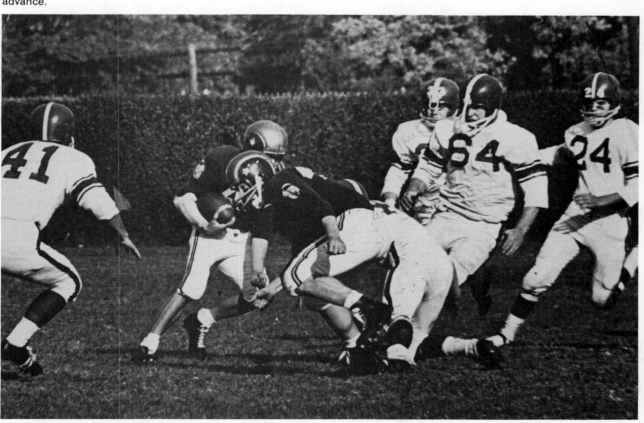

4. If the E releases and the QB drops back, cover the deep outside third.
5. If the ball goes away, cover the deep outside third.

### Safeties

*Alignment:*

Eight to ten yards deep behind the OTs, depending on down and distance.

*Rules:*

1. Key the E or FL to that side and locate the flow of the ball.
2. If the E and FL release: the upside safety covers deep outside third; the backside S covers the deep middle.
3. If the E and FL block and the ball moves laterally: the upside S comes up and plays for the run; the backside S sprints and covers the deep outside half of the field in pursuit.
4. If the E and FL release and there is lateral movement of the ball: the upside S covers the deep outside third; the backside S covers the deep middle.
5. The upside is the side the ball moves toward or a precalled side, usually the wide side of the field; the backside is the opposite side to the upside.

### Safety/Corner Invert

*Alignment:*

When a WR takes a very wide split (10 yards or more) to the upside, or a back goes in motion to the upside, the CB and S will switch assignments.

*Rules:*

1. The CB to the upside will have deep outside responsibility on pass plays.
2. The S will cover the upside flat.
3. If the ball comes, the S comes up to play the run.
4. The CB will run out with the man-in-motion, backing off the LOS to gain depth; the S will come up to play the CB's area.

It is important for every defensive man in the 50 Normal to watch his keys and to find the ball. They will provide greater understanding as to what the offense is doing and what the defensive reaction should be. For example, if a RB goes in motion and there are no WRs, the RB makes that side the upside and the entire team has to know that. If offensive linemen show pass block, everyone reacts; the secondary rush to their pass defense zones and the linemen rush the passer. Football is a game of action and reaction. Training a defensive unit to use different formations and to react in timely fashion will provide your team with dynamic action to stop an offense and get the ball.

# 15

# Goal Line Football

There are a number of special activities that occur near the goal line both offensively and defensively. We will highlight the main objectives of both and establish some general rules to use. It will be wise to remember that there are a wider variety of offensive sets used inside the ten-yard line than anywhere else on the field, many of which are designed to be deceptive and unexpected. Therefore, it requires special defensive preparation to be able to adjust immediately to some strange formation that may not have been seen before.

## GOAL LINE OFFENSE

Naturally, the object is to score. However, a common occurrence in football is to see a team march all the way down the field, first down after first down, only to stall inside the ten and fail to score. One of the reasons for this is the change in defensive strategy that all good teams use near the goal line. Therefore, a good offensive game plan must include plays designed to deal with these different defenses.

The first basic concept to accept is to do the things you do best. If your running game is your strong point, then make it the backbone of your scoring philosophy. If you feel you throw more effectively, then arrange for some special pass plays to get your team into the end zone. Plan them to be versatile enough to use against the toughest of defensive alignments, and practice them often to make their execution as faultless as possible.

The next most important rule is to be simple and basic. Do not try to be fancy, which may require a player or players to do something complicated. In the excitement and pressure that exists near the goal line, players tend to tighten and their performances may falter. Give

GOAL LINE OFFENSE VS DEFENSE. Linemen close gaps
as they both are concerned with penetration by the other.

TOUCHDOWN PLAY. The offense squeezes in tight
together to wedge out running room on a play designed to
have a RB dive over the goal line for a touchdown.

**A**
**TD PLAY
LEFT**

**B**
**POWER I
SLANT LEFT**

them something that requires strength, like a power play into the line or a pass that may deceive or confuse the secondary.

Another rule is to run straight ahead or on slants, but avoid trying to sweep, reverse, or draw near the end zone. Straight shots do not waste any time with the ball carrier behind the LOS where he could be thrown for a loss by a LBR stunt. Sweeps and reverses have RBs running parallel to the LOS, and penetration by any defender can cause loss of yardage. Emotions run high near the goal posts. If a team stops the offense or causes them to lose ground, their emotions will make them tougher to deal with on the next play. Therefore, the offense should strike quickly on isolation plays where they have to overcome a few of the defenders, not the whole team. There are a number of favorite scoring plays that every coach has. Above you will find a few for your consideration.

Both plays above employ similar strategy—using brute power to drive for a few short yards. Put your biggest and strongest offensive linemen in the LG, LT, and LE positions in (A) and your two biggest backs or TEs in the blocking back positions. Put your best power runner in the RB slot and instruct him to bury himself into the LE-LT gap as fast and as hard as he can run. This is the straight-ahead approach.

In (B) above, we're using the angle or down block principle by driving each defender away from the hole and using the two blocking backs in the power I as our lead blockers on the corner. This is the slant approach to scoring on a running play.

It is suggested that running to your left is probably better than to your right when down in close because most defensive units put their best people opposite your right side. Of course, if you have a back who can "fly" it doesn't make too much difference where you run the ball. A fly at the goal line is a leaping, headfirst dive by your RB on a quick hand-off like this:

**POWER I LEFT
BAM "FLY" RIGHT**

In all three running plays, you'll notice a Gap 8 defense with three LBRs. There will be more on this later, but most coaches consider it the toughest to score on. That's why we used it for our favorite scoring plays, reasoning if we can score on that defense, we can score on any defense. Of course, if the defense is too tough for you, be ready to throw a few different passes. If they stop your running game, they may be putting too many men on the LOS and are cheating on their pass protection.

Play action passes are usually the most effective pass plays close to the end zone because they tend to freeze the LBRs and CB/Ss to enable the receivers to get open for a quick pass. The RBs and the QB must really put on a magic show to do this and give the pass the best chance of success.

**RECEIVERS**
**1=PRIMARY**
**2=SECONDARY**
**3=TERTIARY**

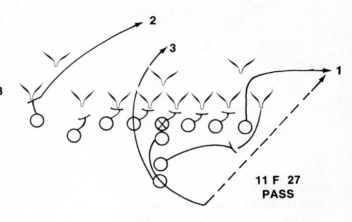

**11 F 27 PASS**

**F2233 BOOTLEG PASS**

A quick reverse pivot by the QB and a low, driving dive into the DT by the FB will create enough diversion for the slot end and slot back to get open. The slot end must drive deep into the end zone to allow room for the slot back to cross the goal line before he cuts for the sideline. The TE drags across the middle, trying to get into a zone vacated by the LS. All linemen "reach" block to their right as the QB gains depth to throw as quickly as he sees a receiver open. If no one puts pressure on him, he may be

able to run the ball into the end zone. His order of priority is from right to left in his search for an open receiver.

Another surprise pass is the quick one to the back flat.

Again the play's success rests on a good QB-RB fake and a quick drop and setup by the QB. The FB must throw a leveling cross-body block on the DE to give the QB better visibility or a chance to run for the TD. A sharp cut by the TE after driving at the LS should get him open for the instant the QB needs to fire the ball to him.

The last pass to be covered is a "gimmick" play, one designed to confuse the defense. It's usually good at least once a game unless you've been well scouted and your opponents know what's coming.

**TD PASS LEFT**

QUARTERBACK BOOTLEG PASS. The QB raises the ball to pass as he rolls out to the right, avoiding the pass rush.

The QB must sprint out to a seven-yard depth, looking at the FL and RB to eye fake the defensive secondary. The LE must make a solid shoulder block on the DT, taking care not to be pushed in toward the middle of the field. By blocking the DT's outside shoulder, he can release quickly to the flat after counting "one thousand one" to give the FL and RB time to clear the defenders out of the flat zone. As soon as the LE crosses the goal line he should cut for the sideline and look immediately for the ball. Once again the FB must cut the DE down to give the QB the pass-run option.

When the team is running through plays on the day before a game, every time they get inside the ten-yard line have them run or throw a play you intend to use to score. Their ability to execute these plays well can sometimes make the difference between a win or a loss.

## GOAL LINE DEFENSE

Player selection for this special team is very important. The coach must assemble the best players at each position to give the goal-line squad the most strength available on the team. Players selected for this team should get special recognition as it should be the most prestigious unit on the team.

The down linemen must be the biggest and strongest players on the team. The DEs from the regular defense should be the best available as should the players from the secondary. Every player has specific responsibilities and keys to follow. They must not be guilty of leaving their assignment unfilled and, by all means, they must be alert at all times for the unexpected, particularly the play action pass plays. The following are a variety of defensive sets.

There are four DTs on our goal-line team and two LBRs. From our basic 50 Normal, two CBs must come out of the game as the two extra DTs go in. The down linemen to the strong side of the offense drop to a four-point stance in the

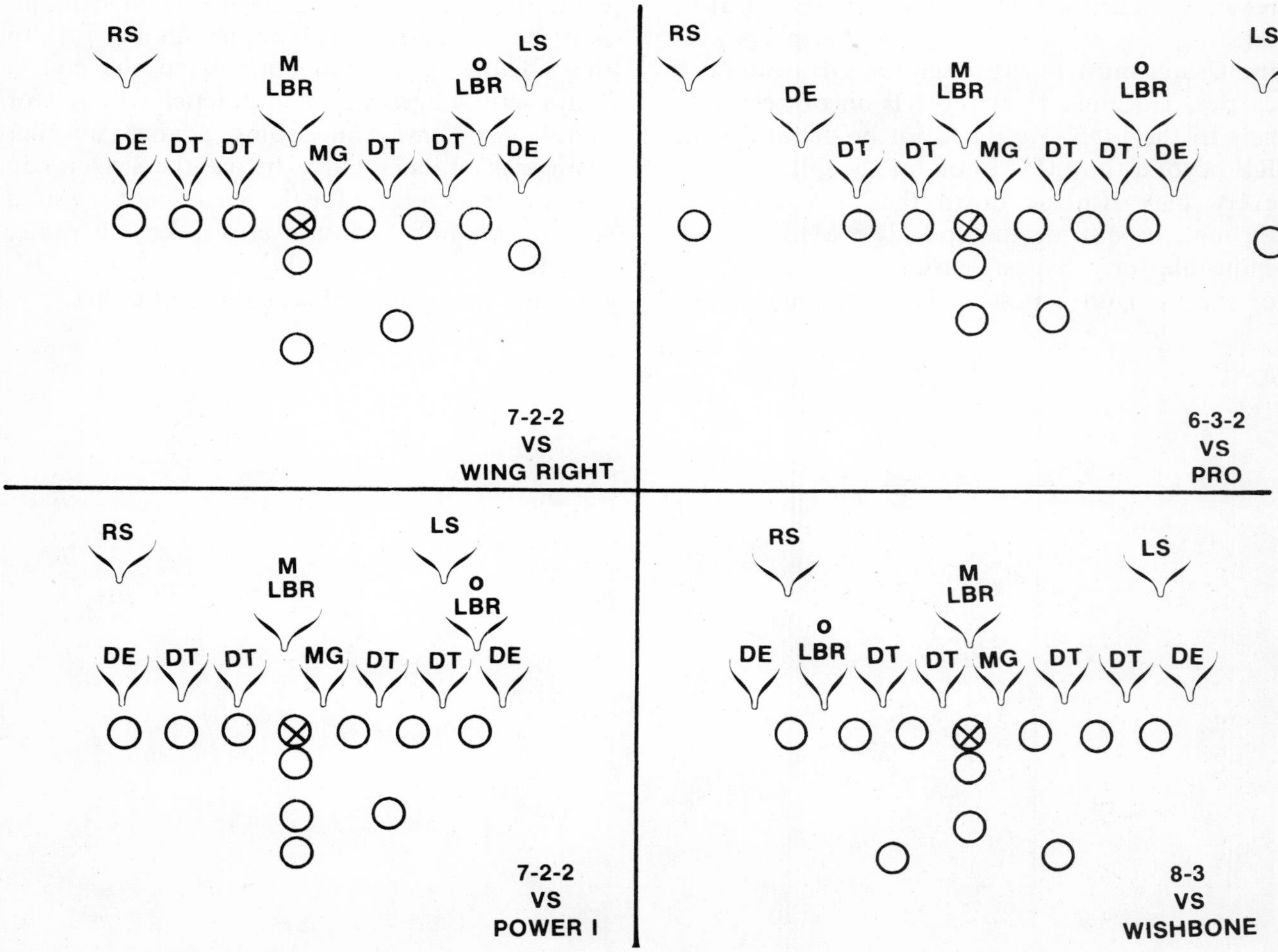

7-2-2
VS
WING RIGHT

6-3-2
VS
PRO

7-2-2
VS
POWER I

8-3
VS
WISHBONE

gaps, while those away from the strength play heads-up from a four-point stance. The gap linemen's job is to penetrate the gap to a two-yard depth and find the ball. The heads-up linemen play through their offensive linemen, fighting the pressure of the block. They must not be moved out of their area. The DEs take a tight three-point stance; their task is to crash on a slant toward the RBs as fast as they can get there. On a pass rush, they must take an outside rush to contain the QB. If the offensive end blocks down, they must quickly fill off his tail. If the end tries to release, from the DE's tight stance he can jam the TE into the DT and not allow him to release untouched.

Safeties must play WRs man to man, staying close to them and looking for quick hook or sharp out patterns. Use the sidelines and the end zone end lines to force the receiver into a restricted area. Play three to four yards off the LOS; try to bump the receiver off his stride before the ball is airborne. Key the WR and react to his actions. If he blocks, come up. If he releases, stay with him. The MLBR plays over the C and must key through the QB to the ball carrier. He must meet the RB on or before he gets to the LOS. He must not be driven by the RB beyond the LOS. Look for the QB sneak on every play. Pursue down the LOS on plays through or outside the end. The MLBR is responsible for a back releasing to the weak side of the field on a pass play. The coach should light a fire under the team and get them to play twice as strong as they really are.

The outside LBR plays inside the DE on the nose of the TE. He must key through the TE to the deep RB. If the TE blocks down, he must come up to play the run. If the TE blocks out, he must fill inside to play the run. When the TE releases, he must jam him and, if there is a WR to his side, play the TE man to man. In a tight formation, cover the flat and any back going to that side. Against the wishbone or full house T, he must play on all fours in the offensive LE-LT gap when the team is using the 8-3 defense. Any offensive spread formation may require the OLBR to move outside and play a man-to-man coverage against a WR. However, if a team has indicated an inclination toward this kind of offense, the coach should replace the OLBR with a CB or a safety to get more speed into his secondary.

A final word: if the offense comes out in an offensive set that the defense may be confused with, the MLBR (the goal-line team captain) must be instructed to call a time out and rush to the sideline to get direction from the coach. Team scrimmages are good practice sessions for goal-line defense, but going against another team in a practice game before the season can give the team a taste for the excitement required for outstanding goal-line effort. Lavish praise on the team whenever they are successful. It's the best coaching technique on the market.

# 16

# The Punt

This special team effort will also be covered in two parts, the receiving team and the punting team. As is true of the kickoff, dealing with the punt must be a major preparation area for the coach. It has an extra ingredient to deal with, the snap from center, which is one of the most feared aspects of the game and frightens every coach. There are many specific assignments that must be carried out if a team is going to successfully execute its punting game. Next to lost fumbles and interceptions, more games are lost on punt plays than any other.

## THE PUNTING TEAM

The selection of personnel for the punt kicking team is probably the most difficult of all the special teams. The coach must find players who are fast, good blockers and good tacklers. A few of them must also be big and strong to resist a concentrated attack designed to block the punt. The coach must consider making special substitutions to remove members of his regular offensive team and to replace them with players more suited to the unique assignments on the punting team. This must be done quickly because it usually happens after a third down fails to make a first down and the clock may be running. If the ball isn't snapped in 30 seconds from the time the referee whistles the ball ready for play, then a five-yard delay of game penalty will be marched off. There are two basic kinds of punt formations—tight and spread.

The tight punt provides stronger protection against a block attempt but weakens the downfield coverage of the punt required to prevent a runback. The spread punt provides better runback defense but does not cope with the punt block as well. However, if the center can get the ball back quickly and the punter gets the ball

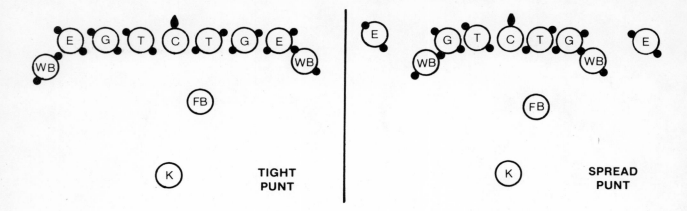

TIGHT PUNT

SPREAD PUNT

away without delay, the spread can be used safely. If either player is average and the defense has a history of block attempts, the coach should favor the tight formation over the spread.

You will notice that the tackles are placed next to the center. The coach should select the fastest of his big tackles from either the offensive or defensive teams to fill these positions. The reason for putting the Ts next to the C is to counter a frequent defensive tactic of attacking the gaps on either side of the C. Match fire power with fire power. Their stance is the same used by all linemen. It is somewhat unique compared to what most coaches use because it is a stand-up rather than a three-point stance. Players to the right of the C stand with their inside (left) legs six inches back and their hands on their knees, while the linemen to the left of the C have their inside (right) legs back using the same stance. There should be not more than six inches between the feet of adjoining linemen. They must remain motionless, but their eyes should roam left and right to make the final decision as to whom they should block.

The blocking priorities for each lineman are: 1) anyone in his inside gap; 2) if no one is there, anyone over (heads up) him; 3) if no one is there either, any LBR behind the man in his inside gap or over him; 4) anyone in his outside gap. The blockers must make the proper determination in the few seconds before the snap of the ball.

When the snap occurs, the T, G, and E on both sides of the C must step forward and in toward the C with their inside legs. They must not lunge or create gaps in the line and must

keep their outside foot well planted to resist the force of the defenders. It is for this benefit that the stand-up stance is used. It provides a stronger foundation against the rush and also reduces the possibility of a defender leaping over a blocker in a three-point stance. In addition, when they hear the ball kicked, they can release more quickly down the field to make the tackle. Their path downfield must be adjusted by the call from the punter—"left," "middle," or "right" when he sees where the ball is going.

The duties of the C have been covered in Chapter 5. The Ts must protect the C as much as possible because he is vulnerable right after he begins to snap the ball. The Gs can be either big, fast guards or fast Ts filling the G spots on the punting team. The Es usually are the fastest of the DEs or may be the best tacklers from the WR group. On occasion, CBs or safeties turn out to be the best because they have more experience at open-field tackling. At any rate, the Es go directly at the punt returner to make the tackle, and the outside responsibility belongs to the wing backs (WB). They, too, can be CBs, safeties, or even good tacklers from the RB crew. The WBs and Es must make contact with the defenders in their blocking responsibility areas on the LOS before releasing downfield because, if they don't, there's a chance an onrushing DE may be able to block the kick. This is a must for anyone in their inside gap, but defenders outside the WB have a long way to go to block a kick and can be ignored.

The fullback (FB) must be the most alert of all the blockers. He has the responsibility of blocking anyone who gets through the front wall of blockers from end to end. When he makes the choice of who he will block, he must go forward to meet the onrusher and not back up or he may back into the kicker. As soon as the kick is away, he must circle the left side of his team and be the safety tackler on that side if the ball carrier breaks into the open. The kicker has the same task to perform to the right side of the field. The FB position can be filled by the offensive FB if he is a good tackler or by any strong, good blocking RB who can tackle well in the open. It is also possible to use a fast LBR or CB in the FB spot.

The development of a punter is a long and tedious affair. Some boys develop a talent for it by virtue of their own practice before or after a season. For this reason, a coach should ask boys to try out for the position and hope to be lucky enough to find someone with ability. Begin with the boys with the most talent; review the following techniques with them:

## Punting Technique

There are many key phases to a punt: the approach steps, the hold of the ball, the drop of the ball, the movement of the kicking leg, the contact of the ball with the foot, and the follow-through. While awaiting the snap to reach his hands, the punter should have his kicking leg about six inches behind his front foot. He should step forward on the front leg to catch the snap, which is the first of his three-step approach. He should be leaning forward slightly at the waist, and his steps should be shorter than his normal stride. As he is taking his steps, he should be moving the ball in his hands to grasp the lower front part of the ball with his opposite hand (opposite to the kicking leg) while his other hand cradles the lower rear right quarter of the ball. The ball should be rotated to place the laces almost to the outside edge of the ball to avoid having them come in contact with the kicking foot.

The arms should be pulled in with the elbows close to the body. The angle of the ball should be slightly canted toward the opposite foot and never be pointed toward the goal line. As the punter comes off his second step, the arms should extend the ball gently forward and begin to lower the hands to the drop position. He should hold the ball until the last possible in-stant to make the drop as short as he can. The angle of the ball must be slightly downward at the front to expose the rear underpart of the ball to the turned-in angle of the kicking foot. Contact should be made by the side of the lace area of the foot, turned slightly inward, into the fattest part of the ball. Under the laces are the strongest bones of the foot; it is this strength, and not the toes, that must propel the ball. The travel of the leg and foot should be in a slight outside-in-and-up arc to create a spinning effect as the foot comes up and across the bottom of the ball. This action causes a spiral which consistently produces longer distances on kicks.

The follow-through must find the foot going up toward the sky while turning toward the opposite shoulder. The turned-down toe at the time of impact should remain down during the finish of the follow-through. The opposite leg actually propels the entire body up and into the ball and continues up until the foot actually comes off the ground. A great deal of practice is required to improve punting ability. The coach

PUNTER'S FOLLOW-THROUGH. With his kicking leg extended as high as it can go, the punter must raise up on his back leg to get full thrust of power into the punt for height and distance.

must make it part of every day's practice program. While the punter is kicking about 15 times a day, the coach should have the punt returners practicing their skills and the center working on improving his snaps. He may also decide to have his kick-coverage players run down under the punts to become experienced in containing the kick returners. Work on the punting game. It may help you win many games.

## THE PUNT RECEIVING TEAM

This special team must be reviewed in two separate sections—the punt-return play and the punt-block play. The same personnel can be used for both plays but their responsibilities are almost all different. The decision as to when to use one play or the other depends on many factors. If the opponent's C has a weak snap or if the punter is slow getting the ball away, a block should be attempted. If they block poorly, have smaller personnel that can be overwhelmed, or use a punting formation that has glaring weaknesses in it, try to block one. If their punter kicks short, a return is not a good bet so try a block. If you're behind late in the game and need a score desperately, send all 11 in after the punter. On the other hand, if they block well, snap well, and quickly get off long kicks, set up your return play and try to break one. If they have slow coverage downfield or have poor tacklers or you have a real speed merchant as a returner, go for the return. Whatever you do, prepare thoroughly for it and be sure the special team members know their jobs well.

### Punt Return Play

There are a number of different plays that can be used to return a punt. There are left side, right side, and middle returns with either "walls" or reverses used to get there. There are also partial or total "hold-up" returns where the receiving team's linemen and LBRs block or hold up the kicking team's linemen to restrain their release downfield to make the tackle. The wall technique requires the return team personnel to retreat to either the left or right, parallel to the sideline and three to five yards apart, to create a protective wall for the ball carrier to run behind. Regardless of which return is used, certain safeguards must always be made to avoid being surprised by the kicking team. The surprises could be an inside run, an outside run, or some kind of pass; the coach must include these possibilities in his punt-return planning.

Selection of personnel on a return play usually includes most of the defensive unit except perhaps for a real speedy back to do the returning. Except for trying to give some two-way players a rest, the coach should try to minimize the number of players coming or going on punt plays. Rather, he should use the kickoff special teams for wholesale substitutions because the clock is stopped and more time can be used for the players to exit or enter the game.

Let's look at a right (or left) side return and the placement of personnel on the field:

**RIGHT SIDE RETURN
(LEFT SIDE OPPOSITE)**

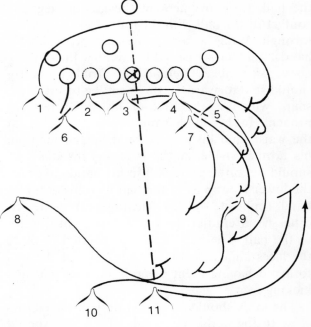

| | | | |
|---|---|---|---|
| 1 | JONES | LE | |
| 2 | SMITH | LT | |
| 3 | WHITE | MG | |
| 4 | BROWN | RT | |
| 5 | BLACK | RE | |
| 6 | CLARK | LLBR | |
| 7 | GREEN | RLBR | |
| 8 | ROBERTS | LCB | |
| 9 | WARNER | RCB | |
| 10 | DAVIS | LS | |
| 11 | SIMPSON | RS | |

*No. 1*

Jones races to a spot about six feet in front of the punter to try to block the kick, looks for a fake with a run to his side, and continues to the opposite side of the LOS, becoming the first block in the wall. If the kicker sets up to pass, No. 1 must holler "pass" to alert his teammates.

*No. 2*

Smith must make his defensive charge into the OT's inside shoulder, which should encourage the OT to release away from the side of the field the return is headed for. The rule for either left or right side returns for all defensive linemen is to charge into the shoulder closest to the side the ball is going to. After making good contact, Smith must retreat across the field and back to his place in the wall, which is about five yards from No. 1.

*No. 3 and No. 4*

White and Brown execute in an identical fashion except that No. 3 follows No. 4 who, in turn, follows No. 5 to their positions on the field. They must look up and down the field to adjust their location in an attempt to keep the wall evenly spaced.

*No. 5*

Black must give their LE a strong bump with a shoulder block to drive him toward the center of the field to get him as far away from the sideline as he can. No. 5 must then race downfield to take his position based on the location of the RCB who is the other end of the wall.

*No. 6*

Clark must not allow their RE to release toward the middle of the field. He should stay inside the RE, shoulder block him to the outside, and run with him to harass him all the way down the field until the whistle blows at the end of the play. He has no wall responsibility.

*No. 7*

Green performs the same effort on the LE after the LE is allowed to release inside by No. 5. Green must prevent their LE from ever getting to the ball carrier as the punt falls from the sky.

*No. 8*

Roberts must prevent anyone near the punt returner from interfering with his catch from retreating to get behind the wall. He must look from side to side to determine who is the "most dangerous man" and then get him.

*No. 9*

Warner is the first block in the wall downfield. His position must be about five yards from where the ball is being caught. If the ball is in the middle or opposite side of the field, he must move while watching the flight of the ball, realizing that the rest of the wall moves with him. If the kick is long, the spacing will be wider, making it more critical for each player to adjust his position carefully.

*No. 10 and No. 11*

Davis and Simpson are twin receivers. Anything to the left side of the field is Davis' ball and anything to the right is Simpson's. Whoever catches the ball must only concentrate on catching it safely. After catching it, he must turn on all his speed to get around the corner to the safety of the wall. For the boy not catching the punt, there are a number of things to do. First he must get in front of his partner and holler "you got it" to leave no doubt as to who is making the catch. Next, he must look at the defenders rushing toward him and decide whether his teammate should make a fair catch or not. A fair catch is a privilege a punt catcher has to enable him to catch the punt without being touched, hit, or tackled by the defense but, in return for this protection, he gives up his right to advance the ball and the right for any teammate to run with the ball. To indicate to the defense that he wants to exercise this privilege, he must raise one arm high over his head and wave his hand from left to right. To avoid having him look downfield to see if the defenders are too close at the same time he's following the flight of the ball, the coach should direct his partner to make the decision. A vocal signal such as "No" or "Stop" or "Catch" should be used to tell him to start waving his arm. Not hearing any call, the punt catcher will assume the return is on and proceed accordingly. The noncatcher must also look for a fumble on the catch and actually be facing the catcher at the instant of impact.

As soon as the catch is made, the blocker must decide how to serve his team in the most effective way. If he feels the returner can make it around the wall, he should lead him around and block the first different color jersey he sees. If there's a doubt he can get behind the wall, the blocker should try to block anyone who may threaten the ball carrier. In this respect, he is serving the same role as No. 8 who is also not assigned to the wall. A word about 8 and 9 and their pass defense responsibility: Although the offensive ends are being hit as they come off the LOS, they may release into a pass route. Before 8 and 9 turn their backs to get into their return assignments, they must be sure a pass is not developing.

Some coaches prefer to have their punt catchers execute a reverse hand-off to confuse the defense. To do this, the player catching the punt must start running away from the wall while his partner, instead of lingering near the punt catcher, must get away from him to the side opposite the wall. The returner catches the ball and begins to run toward his partner, staying on the upfield side (closer to the original LOS) of him. When he gets a few yards away, he moves the ball to the arm closest to his teammate and gently presses it into his stomach. The receiver of the hand-off raises his nearest elbow and closes down on the ball with his other hand and arm to ensure against a disastrous fumble. After getting the ball he must start the race to get behind the wall before he gets tackled. The entire technique is a little more risky but may provide an element of surprise to get the ball carrier on his way to a long run.

The "hold-up" technique can be combined with a wall return or can allow the returner to

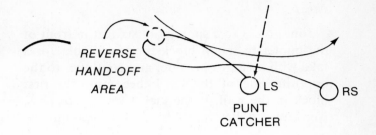

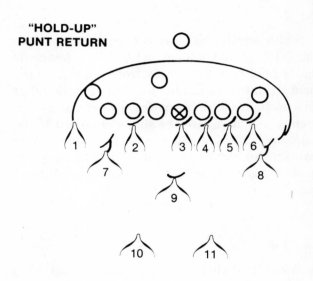

"HOLD-UP" PUNT RETURN

select his own route to the goal line. This approach requires a different placement of personnel on and near the LOS.

Nos. 1, 10, and 11 have the same duties to perform as before. Nos. 2 through 6 actually block their opponents across the LOS to prevent them from releasing downfield. The blocking pressure should be away from the wide side of the field (assume it's to the right) to encourage them to release away from where the ball will be run. Shoulder blocks and/or cross body blocks may be used on the LOS, but only shoulder blocks may be used downfield because of the rule which forbids blocking below the waist on kicks.

Nos. 7 and 8 apply constant pressure on the first defenders to release and must stay with them to the end of the play. Always steer them to the short side of the field.

No. 9 now has the "most dangerous man" responsibility to guarantee the safety of the catch while 10 and 11 do their thing as covered earlier. Overall, the "hold-up" approach is unusual and unexpected and should be used at least once a game. It is particularly good to use if you are going to be catching a punt near your own goal line. The reasoning here is the fewer people going downfield, the better chance you'll have of getting the ball away from your goal line. It also is good against a team with big, slow, clumsy linemen who may get so tangled up, they'll create a huge pile at the LOS and get in their own way. Punt returns require frequent practice because they depend upon many players doing things much different than routine operations. In order to be successful, the coach will have to really work at it and demand strict adherence to his direction. Many coaches make the sacrifice of time and effort and are rewarded handsomely with a number of touchdown runbacks every season.

## Punt Block Play

When the decision is made to set up a punt block, the coach must take stock of his weapons. If he has a superfast player, he should try to set up an outside lane through which this player can get to the kicker to try a block. If he has a quick, big, strong player or players, he should try an interior attack. Lacking either of these major talents, he may have to resort to deception to gain an advantage to block a kick.

As stated earlier, the most frequently attacked area is through either side of the C. Because of the snap technique, the C is a weak link in the blocking wall, particularly at lower levels. Many coaches try to soften the C early in a game by playing the biggest, toughest defensive lineman on him. Unless the C is equally tough, he will begin to anticipate the attacks on him and his effectiveness will be reduced. A common approach through this area is as follows:

**PUNT BLOCK STUNT**

PG. 151

Both DTs, the biggest on the team, are the hole openers for the quickest, biggest LBR. The DT's rule is to make his drive across the head of his opponent to his outside shoulder. This direction will force the blocking lineman to move away from the hole the LBR will rush through. The LBR must stand up with one hand on his DT's backside while all three of them wait for the C to begin his snap. As the LBR starts his charge, he should push his DT's butt out of his way and then leap through the gap into the backfield area. As he approaches the punter, he should cut across his path to the point where he feels the foot will meet the ball. If the LBR touches the ball, he is allowed to make contact with the punter but, if the ball is not touched, any contact with the punter may result in a "roughing the kicker" penalty, which is a disastrous infraction. In some league rules, it results in an automatic first down for the kicking team; in others, it results in a 15-yard penalty, which often gives the kicking team a first down. So, instead of getting the ball, the receiving team actually gives it away, plus valuable yardage.

A more extensive interior blocking scheme involves ten of the eleven punt block team. It actually attempts to exploit several areas on the LOS while maintaining a measure of protection against a surprise by the kicking team. This all-out approach is recommended in situations when it is practically certain that a kick will be made because there is some risk involved if a pass is thrown instead.

**"ALL OUT" PUNT BLOCK PLAY**

PG. 152

## Left Side Attack

No. 1 must, from a stand-up stance, rush to the outside to force the right wing back to pay attention to him. Slight contact through the outside shoulder will tend to open the hole. No. 2 must drive through the inside shoulder of their RE to open the hole and to make contact with him, which should delay his release for a pass. No. 3, the fastest player on the team, must cut sharply behind No. 1's outside move to race through the outside hole.

## Middle Attack

Nos. 4 and 6 drive through the outside shoulders of their opponents, while No. 5 uses the "center pull" technique to nullify his block. This is done by having the DT (No. 5) assume a low squat two-point stance with his arms and hands poised just across the LOS from the C's head. At the snap of the ball, No. 5 raises his arms and hands over the C's head and shoulders and comes down with all the force and strength he can to pull the C down toward the turf. If this cannot be executed successfully, an alternate approach can be made. The DT may attack straight through the C in an attempt to overwhelm him. As long as the C is prevented from closing either gap to his left or right, the DT is doing his job. Meanwhile, LBR types Nos. 7 and 8, from their upright sprinters' starting stances, drive recklessly into each C hole gap for their attack on the punter.

## Right Side Attack

No. 9 must try to tie up two blockers, their LE and left wing back. His initial thrust is into the LE's outside shoulder to widen the inside gap and to prevent the LE from releasing quickly on a pass. After contacting him, the left wing back must be attacked to keep that receiver from releasing. It's a tough job to hit two men on one play but it can be done. No. 10 must use No. 9 as a screen and, as soon as he moves to the outside of the LE, No. 10 should cut into the LE's inside gap and rush toward the punter.

During all of the punt block attacks, No. 11, the punt returner, must be alert to the possibility of a pass by watching the punter carefully for an early indication that a pass is being thrown. When the ball is kicked, he must realize that he is all alone downfield and act accordingly. This is no time for a daring catch or an attempt to scoop up a bouncing ball. If a safe catch can be made, he should avoid being punished by many tacklers by either running out of bounds or diving low into the turf when his forward progress is blocked. With all ten of his teammates involved with the block attempt, he should guarantee possession of the ball.

The coach must execute his punt block plays often in practice to give his players experience. He should also learn where the opponents are most vulnerable and concentrate on that area. A final hint: Watch their C snaps in pregame practice. If they are weak, humpback deliveries, make plans to block a kick.

# 17

# The Kickoff

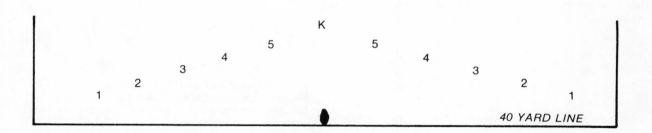

K

5     5

4     4

3     3

2     2

1     1

*40 YARD LINE*

This subject will be divided into two parts, the receiving team and the kickoff team. Both are important to winning football, and coaches must spend enough time to be certain the players know their assignments well. A game can be won or lost on a kickoff, usually because an assignment was missed. Aside from it being a bad way to give up a score, a successful kickoff play can lift a team up by its bootstraps and cause it to play over its head most of the game.

## THE KICKOFF TEAM

As is usually the case on special teams, the selection of personnel is extremely important. There are two primary qualities for kickoff team members: they must be fast, and they must be good tacklers. Practices will provide the coach with many evaluation periods during which he should be able to decide which players have these qualities. Let's take a look at some minor variations of positions on the kickoff team:

No. 1 players should be the fastest players on the team. They must race down the field and go directly to the ball carrier.

No. 2 players are the second fastest and have outside responsibility. They should run at the flag on the goal line and only turn off that course when they are sure that a sideline return or a reverse is not coming their way.

No. 3 players should be bigger than 1 or 2 and be the best tacklers on the team. They run parallel to the sideline and inbounds line and converge on the ball carrier wherever he goes. They are the middle men of the five players on their side of the field and should be cocaptains of the K-O team. Competition between left side and right side should be encouraged.

No. 4 players (linebackers and cornerbacks are good candidates for this spot) are usually in

KICKOFF FORMATION AND KICK. The other ten teammates start to race down the field as a soccer-style kicker approaches the ball from an angle.

PLACEKICKER'S LEG-LIFT. The strong leg of the placekicker must be lifted powerfully as he maintains his balance by leaning back on his other leg; his arms are extended for body control.

the thick of the action because they are near the middle of the field where the ball usually goes. They must stay in their lanes, parallel to the inbounds markers, to make sure that the field is equally protected as they converge on the ball carrier.

No. 5 players should be the biggest guys on the K-O team; they are usually the fastest interior linemen on the entire squad. They have to be the "wall busters" to break up any wedge or wall the receiving team may attempt to use when trying to return up the middle of the field. These two players must sacrifice themselves by destroying the wall with their charge. If they can make the tackle, it's an extra dividend.

The kicker: the search for a kickoff kicker may be a long one for a coach. All boys should be given a tryout, particularly the taller and heavier legged players. Soccer-style kickers do not require the heavy-leg development the straight-on (or conventional) kickers usually have. The placement of the ball on the kickoff tee can affect the flight of the ball. If placed

**TOP VIEW**

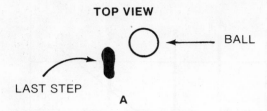

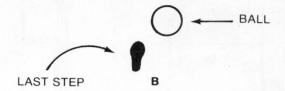

more erect, almost vertical to the ground, a kicked ball will usually travel farther. If tilted back toward a 45-degree angle, it will usually go higher but not as far. Each boy must decide for himself which gives him the best result.

After placing the ball, the straight-on kicker should walk or pace off seven steps, which would bring him to the 33-yard line. The first few steps should be as long as the last ones. An even stride, gaining speed as he nears the ball, will provide the balance and launch pad from which his kicking leg will rise up through the ball. The toe should meet the ball just below the midpoint and the leg should be swung up as though the kicker was trying to put the front of his shoe straight up into the nearest cloud.

If the ball rotates end over end slowly, it's a perfect hit. If it spins rapidly, the ball was hit too close to the bottom. On the other hand, if it floats like a knuckleball, it was kicked at or above the midpoint. To make the required adjustment, the kicker should move the last step of the nonkicking leg either back or forward from the ball.

In A above, the last step is too far forward; the kicking leg will strike the ball too close to the bottom and a short, spinning, end-over-end kick will result. In B, the last step is too far back; the kicking foot will hit too high on the ball and a floater or a topped kick will be made. The correct distance for each boy will vary depending on his stride, so it will be necessary to experiment until the best results are obtained.

The soccer-style kicker approaches the ball from an angle. He must also stride to his starting point, which may be adjusted back from the 40-yard line if his stride doesn't permit him to reach the ball in good rhythm. The major difference between the two kicking styles is the approach angle and the swing of the leg. The soccer-style kicker swings his leg around his body in a wide arc and contacts the ball with the instep above the arch of his foot. As a general rule, his kicks are usually longer, lower, and hook more than the straight-on kicker. The coach must weigh the benefits of one versus the other if there are two boys with similar ability.

After kicking the ball, the kicker must carefully avoid being blocked as he races down the middle of the field. If he and both No. 5 players are blocked, a hole in the defense will provide a long gain possibility and maybe even a touch-

KICKOFF TECHNIQUE. After approaching the ball at a jogging pace, the kicker must contact the ball as he soars upward through the ball for maximum height and distance.

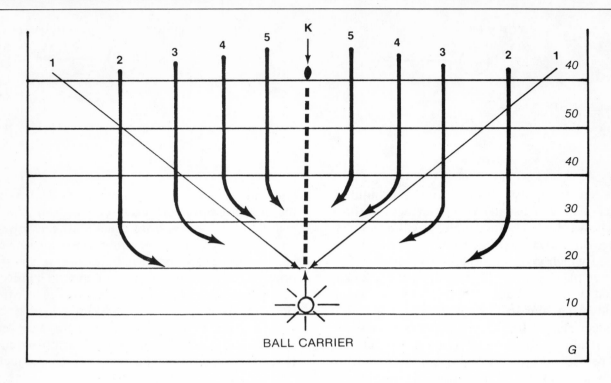

THE KICKOFF TEAM. All of his teammates watch the kicker approach the ball to make sure that he's ahead of them and that they are not offsides.

down. If we put the whole team together, we should get the following pattern as the players race down the field, under control to be able to avoid blockers, to attack the runback attempt.

As the ball carrier moves up the field (assume a middle return for this example), the K-O team converges on the ball. They must be careful not to overrun the ball but should take a pursuit angle that anticipates the speed of the runner to get them into the tackling area. The coach should practice the kickoff with and without a receiving team. A few times each week, it should be a "live" rehearsal with tackling. Don't cheat on preparation in this area.

## KICKOFF RECEIVING TEAM

The goal of every K-O receiving team is to run a kickoff back for a touchdown or at least for a long gain to put the ball in good field position. It is possible to accomplish this fairly often if the coach selects his personnel carefully and if he has them execute their returns in practice at least a few times every week. The requirements for each position are once again different, and players are usually chosen from offensive personnel. If you have a large squad and have a full second offensive team, many of them should be considered for the K-O receiving team. This permits more boys to participate, allows a greater specialization because they can really concentrate on their special duties, and avoids the possibility of injury to first team players. A common formation is:

The front five players must be within the 10-yard area between the 50- and their 40-yard line. It is permissible to have more than five, but no less than five must be in that part of the field. This is designed to keep the team from creating a huge wedge or V-shaped wall farther downfield in front of the ball carrier. Each of the front five should be quick and good open-field blockers. A new rule prohibits blocks below the waist on kicks, so blockers must rely on their speed to get close to the oncoming tacklers and a good shoulder block to stop them or knock them off their feet. Because of the need for speed, slower tackles would not be as desirable as quicker guards. They must assume a semi-crouch stance, being alert to avoid being hit by a low line-drive kick that could bounce off them back into the hands of the kicking team.

The rule covering a free ball on a kickoff states that once the ball passes the 50-yard line, whichever team recovers it, owns it. The front five must always be alert to the "on-side kick" as it is called, particularly when the kicking team is losing near the end of the game. In fact, a wise coach prepares a special receiving team, consisting of superquick, sure-handed receivers and backs to have the best ball handlers on the field in such situations. They should be arranged like this as illustrated in the diagram at top of page 116.

They must be told to fall on the ball and not try to pick it up to return it. Further, if the ball does not cross the 50, the front five must not touch it because the kicking team cannot be

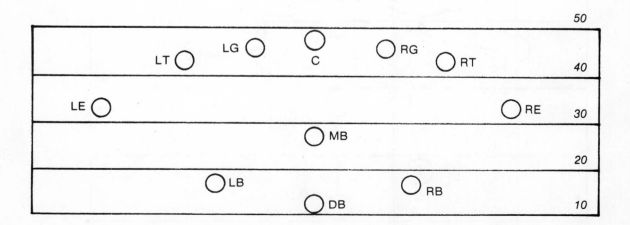

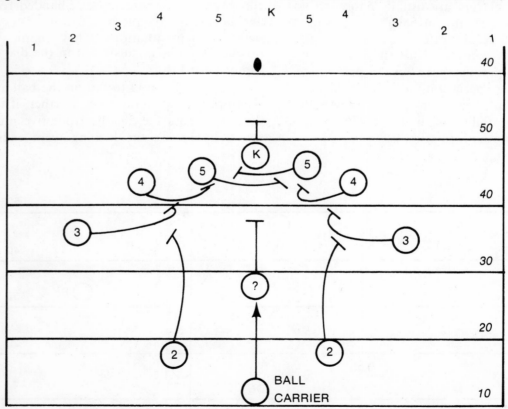

given the ball if they recover it because it did not go the required 10 yards.

The LE and RE must recover any angle kicks toward the sideline or must move quickly into a required blocking position on the field. The middle back (MB), usually a FB, must try to catch short kicks into his area but must never attempt to back up and catch the ball. Rather, he should allow one of the deep backs to come up and catch the ball on the run. Their forward speed will allow them to advance the ball farther. The MB is also the leader of the blocking backfield group and must move into a good blocking position.

The left back (LB), deep back (DB), and right back (RB) all should be the best running backs on the team, with the DB having the greatest speed and the best bet to break away on a long run. They must be instructed to catch any ball in their sector, while running forward, and must avoid reckless attempts to catch a low or a high ball at their feet or over their heads. Any fumble on a kickoff can be a disaster because it will usually result in bad field position.

The two who do not catch the ball must move into blocking position. The closest to the back catching the ball must first look for a fumble on the catch. If there is no fumble, he must turn upfield to block. The ball carrier must quickly follow his blocking, protect the ball in a crowd, and look for a crack of daylight to run through. He should avoid running across the field unless the coach has a right or left side return planned. The most frequently used is the center or "up-the-middle" return that usually gains the most consistent yardage.

One of the best ways to open up the middle is to use a cross-blocking approach to drive the central tacklers toward the sideline. This can be accomplished by matching the numbers of the blockers to the numbers of the K-O team they are assigned to block. It requires a good deal of practice but can be successful.

Either play must attempt to open a seam for the ball carrier. It depends on each blocker, particularly those in the seam area, to get into the right place at the right time. This means anticipating where the tackler will be when the ball carrier gets to the breakthrough area. The

MB must watch the direction of the ball, whether left or right, and move laterally to get in front of the ball when it comes upfield. In both returns, he is the key blocker to help blow open the hole in the defense to spring the running back into the open.

A combined practice drill with the K-O team kicking to the receiving team, allowing everyone to run through their responsibilities, is an excellent weekly activity. It should be done "live" at least a half dozen times in preseason practice to give both teams real gamelike conditions. The coach must also assign backup players, a second string, for both teams. It should be the responsibility of each backup player to make certain that the man he is a substitute for is on the field for his special team assignment. If not, he must rush on the field and take his place. This will avoid the frequent occurrence when only 10 players are on the field, to the embarrassment of the coaching staff.

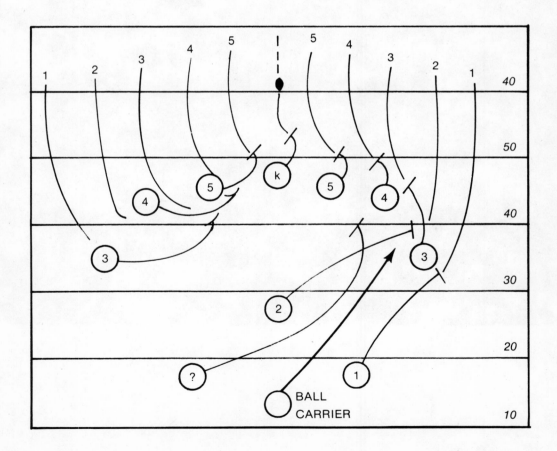

FIELD GOAL UNIT. All blockers stay low and prevent
penetration as the kicker approaches the ball.

# 18

# The Place Kick

Although the use of this special team may be minimal in lower levels, intermediate and higher levels are using the field goal more often as each season passes. And, of course, the extra point is standard operating procedure for many coaches who either find or develop a place kicker with the required ability. Therefore, we will cover all aspects necessary to perform this special team activity successfully, offensively and defensively.

## FG/EP KICKING TEAM

Both of these teams operate from the same basic formation and use the same techniques. Therefore, we will treat them as one—the kicking team. The coach begins with player selection that can parallel the choice of players used on the punting team. He must find the biggest and strongest linemen from either the offensive or defensive teams. A significant difference from the punting team is that the players need not be fast runners, so the coach can pick players based simply on size and strength. Additionally, he can replace the ends with DT types to increase the blocking strength on the LOS. In the wingback positions, the coach again can go for the biggest backs, regardless of speed, or if he lacks boys of this caliber, he can again choose linemen of superior size and strength.

The kicking formation is practically the same as the punting formation except that the fullback is replaced by the holder and the formation is always tight.

The linemen use the upright, two-point stance with their hands on their knees and their inside legs back about six inches. The WBs are tucked in behind the Es and are almost turned sideways facing the sidelines. They must prevent anyone from entering their inside gaps and, if no one attacks that area, they should look to block

## PLACE KICK FORMATION

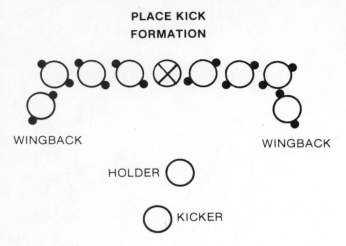

WINGBACK                    WINGBACK

HOLDER

KICKER

anyone rushing around them. Usually a good, hard shoulder block will suffice to break their stride and slow them down. As in the punt, the linemen step up with their inside legs on the snap and lower their shoulders into the onrushing defenders. Their forward step should be long enough to allow the other foot to be far enough behind them to serve as a strong support to keep from being driven back into the kicker.

The selection of the holder frequently is made from the wide receivers or quarterbacks, because they usually have the best hands for handling the ball. It is the primary skill the holder must have; the coach must try many players before he begins to train the best ones. The stance most often used is with the rear knee down parallel to the kicking tee (about 12 inches away) and the front leg extended pointing straight at the C. The holder should actually be sitting on his rear leg's calf and should be holding his extended arms, with hands wide open, toward the C.

Upon catching the snap from center, the holder must quickly bring it down, stand it upright on the tee, spin the ball around to have the laces face the goal posts, and gently but firmly hold the top of the ball with either the forefinger or the palm of the left hand. The important thing for all of this is for the holder to do it quickly and efficiently, and to make sure the ball is as perpendicular as it can be. In other words, the ball must not lean in any direction. If it should be tilted to the left or

right (as the kicker sees the ball), the ball will fly in those directions and probably miss going through the goal posts. If it is allowed to lean back toward the kicker, it will cause the kick to go high but not as far. This is not a problem on extra points, but on field goals it can shorten the distance of the kick which may cause a miss.

The center's snap must be hard and low, trying to hit the holder's outstretched hands with a perfect spiral. This usually gets the ball there more quickly and makes it easier to catch. With a little experimenting, a C can become so methodical he may be able to make the laces arrive in the holder's hands to avoid requiring him to spin the ball to get the laces facing forward. The entire routine between the C and the holder must really be practiced often to make it automatic. A stopwatch should be used to see if the kick can be airborne within 2.0 seconds, which is considered safe for up to high school levels. College and professional teams can usually do it in 1.5 seconds. Naturally, the quicker the kick is made, the less time the defense has to block it.

## PLACE KICKING TECHNIQUE

There are two basic techniques to place kicking from a straight-on approach style of kicking. One requires only one step to be taken before kicking the ball, while the other is a two-step approach. In the one-step routine, the

PLACE KICK STANCE. Kicker leans forward on his kicking foot, arms hanging loosely with his head down as his eyes focus on spot where the holder will place the ball.

PLACE KICKER'S FOLLOW-THROUGH. With knee and ankle locked, the leg swings upward from the hip as the foot thrusts toward the sky.

PLACE KICKER'S CONTACT. After planting his left foot equal to the back of the kicking tee, the kicker contacts the ball about one-third up from the bottom with his eyes fixed on that spot.

PLACE KICK, FOLLOW-THROUGH. After contact, kicker must lift his kicking foot toward the sky and raise up on his rear foot for maximum power and height.

kicker stands with his kicking foot (let's assume he's rightfooted) a shoe length ahead of his back foot. He leans forward at the hip with his arms dangling loosely at his sides and his head lowered with his eyes fixed on the kicking tee. His distance from the tee should be equal to a long, leaping stride which would bring the front of his left shoe equal to the back of the tee. When he peers forward to see the ball arrive in the holder's hands, he shifts his weight with a short jab step on his right foot, takes the long, leaping stride with his left, and starts his kicking leg forward into the ball.

At the time of impact, his ankle and knee must be locked as though there were only one bone in his entire leg from the hip to the big toe. The toes on his kicking foot should be bent upward to apply as much contact to the front of his shoe as possible. The ball must be contacted, as in the kickoff, just below the midpoint of the ball. This will produce the longest kicks, and the leg lift follow-through will elevate the ball over the incoming linemen and the cross bar of the goal posts. After the ball is kicked, the kicker must keep his head down with his eyes fixed on the ground. This will prevent any impairment of his leg lift and follow-through that could be caused by raising his head and neck to see the ball. From the time he is poised waiting for the snap, he should have a mental picture of the goal posts in his head. As he follows through, he should again visualize his leg splitting the middle of the goal posts as he swings his foot straight up into the sky.

Two coaching points: 1) Whether you use the two-inch tee, which gets the ball up higher and is better for extra points, or the one-inch tee, which makes the ball go farther but not as high, be sure the kicker places the tee carefully on the ground about seven yards behind the ball. Also make sure it is pointing straight at the goal posts so that it may be used as a gun sight to aim the kick with. 2) Be sure the kicker is driving his kicking leg straight ahead at the goal posts and does not swing it on an arc that will cause the foot to loop slightly toward the sideline. This can cause a misdirected kick by either hooking or slicing the ball to the left or right. A special square-toe kicking shoe can also be a big help to make the placekicking a vital part of your offense.

## FIELD GOAL/EXTRA POINT BLOCK PLAY

Many of the kick-blocking techniques used on punt blocks can also be used to block place kicks. However, due to the absence of the need to field the kick, an all-out attack on the kick can be launched. The plan must include some deception and some brute strength, and both must be done with good timing and speed.

Any attempt to block a kick cannot afford to lose even a split second of time. Therefore, all players on or near the LOS must keep their eyes fixed on the ball. As soon as they see the C start his snap, they must start across the LOS en route to the kicking area. Let's look at our plan as to how to block a kick.

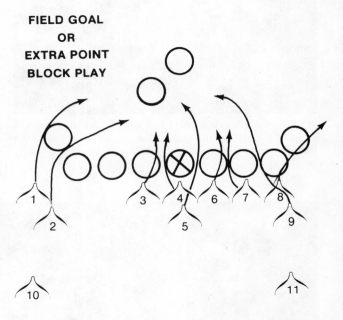

FIELD GOAL
OR
EXTRA POINT
BLOCK PLAY

No. 1 must attempt to draw the RWB out to allow No. 2 to enter the important inside gap. It may be necessary to have 1 charge through the WB's outside shoulder to actually drive open the gap for 2 to race through.

Nos. 3 and 4 should assume shoulder-to-shoulder stances to drive through the C-G hole. This is a brute strength approach trying to get their combined strength simultaneously into the gap. Nos. 6 and 7 line up "heads-up" the LG and LT, but also try to hit one hole with all the force they can muster. However, as No. 6 charges across the LG's head toward the G-T hole, he will divert the LG's attention away from the LBR, No. 5, who is trying to penetrate the C-LG hole. Have the LBR line up directly behind No. 4 but with his feet facing No. 3. This will create the impression that he's going through the RG-C gap but, as No. 4 slants into that hole, No. 5 pivots and rushes through the C-LG hole. He should be the quickest and strongest of the LBR corps and is the primary attack weapon of the team.

Nos. 8 and 9 try a little deception, too. As 8 charges the LE's outside shoulder, No. 9 tries to slant into the LE's inside gap. To make this more deceiving, No. 9 must appear to be ready to attack the LWB, with his toes facing the sideline in a stand-up two-point stance but with his head turned to see the ball move.

Nos. 10 and 11 are pass defenders because there is always a chance the kicking team may try to throw a pass. Because FGs are attempted near the goal line, the likelihood of a pass is ever present. If the distance from the goal is at the outer limit of the kicking team's range, a pass is more likely. If it is windy or raining so as to reduce the possible success of a kick, a pass should be expected. At any rate, if Nos. 10 and 11 are ready, they will discourage the pass because the element of surprise will not be present. Passes on fake extra-point plays are even more common, particularly if a two-point conversion is necessary to tie or win the ball game, or if the offensive team has not shown any consistency kicking the ball through the goal posts. Nos. 10 and 11 should observe the WBs and Es after the snap of the ball. If a pass is planned, they will try to release into the secondary. Nos. 2 and 8 should be alert to this possibility, too, and if they see their E trying to release, they must try to hold him up to delay his release. Meanwhile, everyone else will be rushing the passer and there shouldn't be much time to throw the ball.

The coach should try to combine the offensive and defensive field-goal teams to practice kicking against a live defense and to let the defense try to block a live kick. Special practice segments like this often seem to divert valuable time away from other important practice activity, but a wise coach will find that it pays to be prepared in both of these areas. Make time for this kind of practice, because it can win ball games for you.

COACH'S GAME-TIME MEETING. Players gather around
the coach to adjust to a change in strategy.

# 19

# From One Coach to Another

Coaching is a great profession. It will give you an opportunity to experience many challenges, emotions, and satisfactions. It requires total involvement and dedication—an investment of your time and energy. You will be expected to do a thorough job of planning, instructing, and directing the team to the heights their ability will allow them to achieve. It's an opportunity not many people have, and one that must not be taken lightly. We would like to review with you some major areas that coaches get involved in to enable you to benefit from our experiences.

## OBJECTIVES

Players of any game want to win. You must help them prepare for winning by performing your role completely. Preparation is the key word for coaching. We have covered many aspects of preparation but there are many more for you to add to your play book. Always remember that a team consists of starters and substitutes; it's the coach's duty to see that all team members participate whenever he feels they may be able to. It will make the entire squad into a team, and it takes a team to win.

## MOTIVATION

There are an assortment of techniques available to a coach to spur his players on to greater achievements. Be free with your praise; use the "pat on the back" approach. If a boy does one out of two things badly, compliment him for the good performance; he will criticize himself for the bad one. But, don't forget to constructively critique his effort so that he knows why he performed poorly. The best way to get boys to produce is to reward them for their effort. Winning is the best reward but praise for wholehearted effort is always available to the coach, even when winning may not be.

## COUNSELING

A coach is often referred to as a father on the field. Football players are a somewhat unique breed because they mix strength, speed, energy, and intelligence with pain, sweat, anxiety, and dedication to produce a team. But, despite all those virtues, players are sensitive to peer pressure and a failure of teamwork with their team members. Good teams are usually close-knit teams where most boys get along with everyone on the team. A coach must be aware of any situation that may disrupt team unity and must provide the necessary guidance and advice to keep the boys in harmony. If a boy needs attention, give it to him in privacy and be gentle with him. The era of the iron-handed coach is over. Make every boy feel that he is as important as anyone on the team and that there is only one standard for behavior. Establish the rules for team conduct at the start of the practice season, and administer them faithfully and fairly. Remember, you are a coach and a father image to every boy on your team.

## GOALS

If there is to be improvement, there must be both team goals and personal goals. The coach must determine what the targets should be and then help in every way to reach them. Individual goals may involve strength, weight, speed, and performance. These goals must be realistic in order to be true tests of dedication. Team goals may be pass interceptions, fumble recoveries, and so on, on defense; and pass completions, first downs, and so on, on offense. There are dozens available in all areas of the sport; the coach should set up statistics, wall charts, posters, and the like to identify what they are and how the performances stack up against them.

## LOYALTY

The team is the most important single ingredient in any sport. This is an accepted concept among coaches. To ensure that your team is the focal point, you must encourage sacrifice and loyalty for the good of the team. An example of this is attendance at team practice sessions. Players can find a number of seemingly valid reasons for missing practice and, if that becomes a common occurrence, it will hurt the team's chances for success. By encouraging sacrifice for the good of the team, attendance will be excellent and everyone will be prepared when the opening whistle is blown. The coach must set unyielding, rigid rules for team activities and accept only a doctor's or a parent's note as a valid excuse for failing to attend an activity. Team captains should be selected (not elected) to ensure that good examples of loyalty and leadership qualities are out in front of the team for everyone to see.

## PLANNING

In the coaching profession, planning means a wide variety of things. It begins before the season when decisions must be made as to what kind of offensive and defensive formations will be used. A selection of plays from the play book must be made, a few at a time, to avoid laying too much on the boys at once. As the season progresses, plays that have succeeded should be retained and those that failed should be discarded. Defensive plans should be made by making an outline of the steps you plan to take to teach the boys what each position's responsibilities are. If they don't know where to line up and what they must guard against, their execution will suffer because they'll be thinking instead of reacting.

A planning calendar should be made to outline what you want to accomplish at each practice, including the number of minutes allotted to each activity. The best way to demoralize a team is to appear confused and unprepared. This applies to all coaches, so your planning must be segregated into what each assistant coach must do and with which players. Give your assistants specialized areas to work in (for example, offense, defense, special teams, equipment, and so on).

## EQUIPMENT

Equipment is extremely important. Never try to compromise the quality of football equipment. Good equipment protects better and lasts longer. Be very attentive to sizes and fit. For example, loose helmets can cause injury rather than prevent it. We have seen severely bruised noses caused by loose helmets coming down over a boy's eyes. Shoulder pads that are too small will not protect the upper arms or points of the shoulders. Pants that are too big will cause the thigh pads to rest on the knees and not avoid painful upper-leg bruises. There are countless other examples. Therefore, it is extremely important that a competent individual be given the task of obtaining, maintaining, and distributing the gear required to support a football team. Special attention must also be given to day-to-day repairs to ensure that no player goes on the field unprotected by using defective gear. Reconditioning and repair at the end of the season will result in the storage of reissuable equipment at the start of the next season.

## MEDICAL

A coach must be certain that all medical aspects are covered. A physical examination must be given to each boy before he's allowed to participate in a single practice. A parent's permission slip has to be provided and signed to allow a boy to join a team. Thereafter, proper medical, first-aid supplies must be on hand at every practice and game. It is strongly recommended that a doctor be on hand for each game, and that at least one of the coaches have first-aid experience to provide coverage at practice. Be extremely attentive to head injuries and joint injuries. If a boy is injured in any way, be safe and get him to qualified medical people for examination. Don't take any chances; the welfare of the boys is in your hands.

## ATTENDANCE

A football program must be efficiently managed, and the coach is the manager. He must keep attendance records of each practice and talk to boys who have excessive absences. We always allowed two unexcused absences per season (we covered excused absences earlier); on the third occasion, the boy was routinely dropped from the squad. Without explicit, uncompromisable rules like this, a boy may take liberties that will be bad for him and the team. All rules for behavior must be clearly stated.

## PUBLICITY

Arrangements should be made for team publicity. The success of many leagues and teams can be attributed to an attentive policy of letting the surrounding community know about the team's activities. Schools often select students aspiring for journalistic careers to serve as reporters for their teams. Local newspapers usually are pleased to cooperate with dependable personnel to print the accomplishments of the team and its players. To be realistic, we must recognize that a football field is a stage upon which twenty-two players perform. We have always believed that players deserve to be recognized for their efforts. It's part of the reward for playing and can often promote future team participation as youngsters follow the team's progress in the newspapers and look forward to when they are old enough to play. Be sure to spread the praise around to encourage as many players as possible.

## TEAM MANAGER

A team manager is a necessity. He is often a boy in the same age group as the team and may be someone who doesn't aspire to play but wants to be associated with the team. His duties include having the footballs, water pails, extra equipment, adhesive tape for strapping ankles, first-aid kit, kicking tees, equipment repair kit, and other essentials available at the field for every practice and game. He is invaluable to the smooth functioning of the team and is as important as any coach and any player. Be sure to choose the right boy and be sure to praise him frequently for a job well done. Don't let the players abuse him; insist on his involvement with all team activities including dinners, awards, etc.

## INDIVIDUAL CAREER PATHS

In the early chapters we went into the criteria generally used to determine which position a boy is best suited for. This is but another of the coach's responsibilities, one that may have a lasting impact on a player's career. After the initial decision is made, the coach must constantly evaluate his players' performances and look for situations where a position change may be warranted. There are a few points to be underscored. The coach must assemble the best team he can put on the field. If he doesn't, he will lose games and lose the respect of players, parents, and supporters. However, in the process he should try to be mindful of the desires of the boys, too. Someone playing in a position that he has little or no interest in may soon become a poor performer because his heart is not in it.

On the other hand, it may be possible for the coach to change a player's attitude through encouragement and by stressing his importance to the team. Usually young players aspire to be QBs or RBs or other more glorified positions. Interior linemen are looked upon as faceless and nameless players in some people's opinions. Obviously a team cannot function without solid performers in those positions. This area must be given special attention by a coach, because it is the most likely place for problems to arise.

Sometimes it may be necessary for the coach to experiment in his attempt to convince boys that they are not capable of playing a position of their choice. Use your practice periods to do this. For example, if a boy thinks he can be a QB, let him throw passes in the pass practice drill. This will usually resolve the matter. If the boy is a marginal passer, give him a few days to try out. In some instances you may end up with someone who doesn't fit the original mold and may be able to double as a backup QB.

The experiment routine should also be used when you initiate the position change. You may suddenly need a receiver and think that a certain boy may be able to do the job. We strongly urge all experiments be done as discreetly as possible. It may be a little inconvenient to keep a few boys until after practice is over and all of the team is dismissed to hold your special tryout, but it would be worth it. You must always be mindful of peer pressure and the inherent fear that many youngsters have of failure. If your receiver candidate drops every pass thrown to him, at least it would be in private; he would not be subjected to teasing from some of his heartless teammates.

Perhaps the biggest decision a coach must face in this area concerns the future career path of a player. The question a coach must ask is "Will this boy be able to play this position in the future?" The next level up may be senior high school for a boy on a junior high team. The coach should try to envision the progress a player can make in size, ability, and in intangibles like dedication, loyalty, hustle, etc. In other words, don't only concern yourself with today but try to look to tomorrow. This is particularly true of your top players. We must realize that many positions require a broad base of experience and skill development. If we keep a boy in a position he isn't likely to play in the future, we are impacting his personal development. It obviously isn't always possible to get high scores in this effort, but a good coach must give it attention and consideration.

## WINNING RESPECT

A team is at its best when everyone's attitude is healthy and there is good rapport between the players and their coach. It is important that the coach win the respect of his players. In addition to all of the psychological aspects covered in this last chapter, the boys must respect the coach for his knowledge of the game and the personal dedication he applies in running his football program. The longer you serve as coach, the more competent you should become. There are many ways you can learn more about the game. Make every attempt to see as many games as possible. Go to local high school games; watch the college and professional teams on television. Always have a pad and pencil ready to diagram something you see that you never saw before. Many upper-level coaches are

HALFTIME STRATEGY. The coach reviews the first half's experiences and explains to his QB the things he wants changed in the second half.

there because they are innovative and imaginative in their offensive and defensive strategy. You can pick up their secrets by following their game plans and strategy.

Make a special effort to see teams play in your own league to become aware of what their strengths and weaknesses are. We won many games because we scouted the opposition and developed our plan of attack based on what we felt were their most vulnerable areas. If you can't personally see them play, arrange for an assistant or some other competent interested person to do it. Be sure they diagram offensive plays and formations and defensive alignments, too. Notes should also refer to outstanding players on both offense and defense to permit special preparations to cope with them. We also have used tape recorders on our scouting jaunts and described everything we saw for later reference when we transcribed the playback on our pads. Special plans should then be prepared and

reviewed with the team. Their reaction to your extensive effort will be one of admiration and respect because they will see how much effort you have expended on their behalf.

## COMMITMENT

It has been particularly gratifying for me to meet a former player who went on to play football in college and hear him comment on how much more we did in our coaching activity compared to what he encountered in college. Our philosophy has always been that players are with you for a short span of time, perhaps only one or two years. Their football careers are in your hands. If you don't feel you owe them all you can possibly do for them, then perhaps coaching is not for you. You must feel a compelling desire to give them every opportunity to succeed. If you follow this code, you'll win many games you would have otherwise lost. There is no greater sense of accomplishment than to win the tough ones; and conversely, the depths of despair engulf you when you lose because down deep in your heart you feel that, through your oversight, some aspect of the game wasn't properly prepared for. Not unlike a general, you are bearing the weight of command, and with it goes the responsibility for your men. And like that general, the fruits of victory are yours not merely because you won but because you cared enough to do your very best for the youngsters who depended on you for leadership and intelligence.

## CONCLUSION

Your job is to make football a rewarding experience for your players. Try to make it fun; don't deprive them of any activity that may be necessary for them to improve. Make them stretch to the limit of their ability and, when they achieve that, make them reach out again for greater heights. Help them recover from setbacks by showing your confidence in their ability. No matter how old they are, treat them with respect and courtesy. Be an example for them to look up to and admire by being everything a coach should be to his team.

# Index